Warning to the West

Alexander Solzhenitsyn

WARNING TO THE WEST

Farrar, Straus and Giroux · New York

Printed in the United States of America
DESIGNED BY HERB JOHNSON

FIRST EDITION, 1976

Library of Congress Cataloging in Publication Data
Solzhenitsyn, Aleksandr Isaevich, 1918–
    Warning to the West.
    Consists of speeches given to the Americans and to the British
from June 30, 1975 to March 24, 1976.
    1. Russia—Politics and government—1917–   —Addresses, es-
says, lectures. 2. Russia—Foreign relations—United States—Ad-
dresses, essays, lectures. 3. United States—Foreign relations—
Russia—Addresses, essays, lectures. 4. Russia—Foreign relations
—Great Britain—Addresses, essays, lectures. 5. Great Britain—
Foreign relations—Russia—Addresses, essays, lectures.
DK266.S5584   320.9′47′085   76–24467

Mr. Solzhenitsyn's American speeches were translated by Harris
L. Coulter and Nataly Martin, and edited for this edition by
Alexis Klimoff

10 9 8 7 6 5

Contents

Speeches to the Americans

[*JUNE* 30, 1975]

INTRODUCTION BY GEORGE MEANY

When we think of the historic struggles and conflicts of this century, we naturally think of famous leaders: men who governed nations, commanded armies, and inspired movements in the defense of liberty, or in the service of ideologies which have obliterated liberty.

Yet today, in this grave hour in human history, when the forces arrayed against the free spirit of man are more powerful, more brutal, and more lethal than ever before, the single figure who has raised highest the flame of liberty heads no state, commands no army, and leads no movement that our eyes can see.

But there is a movement—a hidden movement of

human beings who have no offices and no head-
quarters, who are not represented in the great halls
where nations meet, who every day risk or suffer
more for the right to speak, to think, and to be
themselves than any of us here are likely to risk in
our entire lifetime.

Where are the members of this invisible move-
ment? As we prepare tonight to honor the presence
of one of them among us, let us give some thought
to the rest: to the millions who are trapped in Soviet
slave-labor camps; to the countless thousands
drugged and strait-jacketed in so-called insane asy-
lums; to the multitudes of voiceless workers who
slave in the factories of the commissars; to all those
who strain for bits and pieces of truth through the
jammed frequencies of forbidden broadcasts, and
who record and pass outlawed thoughts from hand
to hand in the shadows of tyranny.

But if they remain invisible to us, we can hear
them now, for there has come forth from under the
rubble of oppression a voice that demands to be
heard, a voice that will not be denied.

We heed this voice, not because it speaks for the
left or the right or for any faction, but because it
hurls truth and courage into the teeth of total power
when it would be so much easier and more com-

fortable to submit and to embrace the lies by which that power lives.

What is the strength of this voice? How has it broken through to us when others have been stilled? Its strength is art.

Alexander Solzhenitsyn is not a crusader. He is not a politician. He is not a general. He is an artist.

Solzhenitsyn's art illuminates the truth. It is, in a sense, subversive: subversive of hypocrisy, subversive of delusion, subversive of the Big Lie.

No man in modern times and very few in all of history have demonstrated as drastically as Alexander Solzhenitsyn the power of the pen coupled with the courage to free men's minds.

We need that power desperately today. We need it to teach the new and the forgetful generations in our midst what it means not to be free. Freedom is not an abstraction; neither is the absence of freedom. Solzhenitsyn has helped us to see that, thanks to his art and his courage.

His art is a unique gift. It cannot be transmitted to another. But let us pray that his courage is contagious.

We need echoes of his voice. We need to hear the echoes in the White House. We need to hear the echoes in the Congress and in the State Department and in the universities and in the media, and if you please, Mr. Ambassador Patrick Moynihan, in the United Nations.

The American trade-union movement, from its beginnings to the present, has been dedicated to the firm, unyielding belief in freedom. Freedom for all mankind, as well as for ourselves. It is in that spirit that we are honored to present Alexander Solzhenitsyn.

MOST of those present here today are workers. Creative workers. And I myself, having spent many years of my life as a bricklayer, as a foundry-man, as a manual worker, in the name of all who have shared this forced labor with me, like the two Gulag prisoners whom you just saw,* and on behalf of those who are doing forced labor in our country, I can start my speech today with the greeting: "Brothers! Brothers in Labor!"

And not to forget the many honored guests pres-

---

* Alexander Dolgun and Simas Kudirka.

Mr. Solzhenitsyn delivered this speech in Washington, D.C., at a dinner which was given in his honor by the AFL-CIO and hosted by George Meany, the union's president.

ent here tonight, let me add: "Ladies and gentle-men."

"Workers of the world, unite!" Who of us has not heard this slogan, which has been sounding through the world for 125 years? Today you can find it in any Soviet pamphlet as well as in every issue of *Pravda*. But never have the leaders of the Communist Revolution in the Soviet Union used these words sincerely and in their full meaning. When so many lies have accumulated over the decades, we forget the radical and basic lie which is not on the leaves of the tree but at its very roots.

It is now almost impossible to remember or to believe . . . For instance, I recently reprinted a pamphlet from the year 1918. This was a detailed record of a meeting of all representatives of the factories in Petrograd, the city known in our country as the "cradle of the Revolution."

I repeat, this was March 1918, only four months after the October Revolution, and all the representatives of the Petrograd factories were denouncing the Communists who had deceived them in all their promises. What is more, not only had the Communists abandoned Petrograd to cold and hunger, themselves having fled from Petrograd to Moscow, but they had given orders to open machine-gun fire on the crowds of workers in the factory courtyards who were demanding the election of independent factory committees.

Let me remind you, this was March 1918. Scarcely anyone now can recall the other, similar acts: the crushing of the Petrograd strikes in 1921, the shooting of workers in Kolpino in the same year . . .

At the beginning of the Revolution, all those in the leadership, the Central Committee of the Communist Party, were émigré intellectuals who had returned after disturbances had already broken out in Russia to carry out the Communist Revolution. But one of them was a genuine worker, a highly skilled lathe operator until the last day of his life, Alexander Shliapnikov. Who is familiar with that name today? And yet it was he who expressed the true interests of the workers within the Communist leadership. In the years before the Revolution it was Shliapnikov who ran the whole Communist Party in Russia—not Lenin, who was an émigré. In 1921, he headed the Workers' Opposition, which charged that the Communist leadership had betrayed the interests of the workers, that it was crushing and oppressing the proletariat and had degenerated into a bureaucracy.

Shliapnikov disappeared from sight. He was arrested later, and since he firmly stood his ground he was shot in prison; his name is perhaps unknown to most people here today. But I remind you: before the Revolution the head of the Communist Party of Russia was Shliapnikov—not Lenin.

Since that time, the working class has never been able to stand up for its rights and, in contrast to all the Western countries, our working class receives only handouts. It cannot defend its simplest, everyday interests, and the least strike for pay or for better living conditions is viewed as counter-revolutionary. Thanks to the closed nature of the Soviet system, you have probably never heard of the textile strikes in 1930 in Ivanovo, or of the 1961 worker unrest in Murom and Alexandrovo, or of the major workers' uprising in Novocherkassk in 1962 —this was in Khrushchev's time, well after the so-called thaw.

The story of this uprising will shortly be told in detail in my book, *The Gulag Archipelago*, III. It is a story of how workers went in peaceful demonstration to the Novocherkassk party headquarters, carrying portraits of Lenin, to request a change in economic conditions. They were fired on with machine guns and dispersed with tanks. No family could even collect its wounded and dead: all were taken away in secret by the authorities.

I don't have to explain to those present here that in our country, ever since the Revolution, there has never been such a thing as a free trade union.

The leaders of the British trade unions are free to play the unworthy game of paying visits to imaginary Soviet trade unions and receiving odious visits in return. But the AFL-CIO has never given in to these illusions.

The American workers' movement has never allowed itself to be blinded and to mistake slavery for freedom. And today, on behalf of all of our oppressed people, I thank you for this!

In 1947, when liberal thinkers and wise men of the West, who had forgotten the meaning of the word "liberty," were swearing that there were no concentration camps in the Soviet Union at all, the American Federation of Labor published a map of our concentration camps, and on behalf of all of the prisoners of those times, I want to thank the American workers' movement for this.

But just as we feel ourselves your allies here, there also exists another alliance—at first glance a strange and surprising one, but if you think about it, one which is well-founded and easy to understand:

this is the alliance between our Communist leaders and your capitalists.

This alliance is not new. The very famous Armand Hammer, who flourishes here today, laid the basis for this when he made the first exploratory trip to Soviet Russia in Lenin's time, in the very first years of the Revolution. He was extremely successful in this reconnaissance mission and ever since then, for all these fifty years, we see continuous and steady support by the businessmen of the West for the Soviet Communist leaders. The clumsy and awkward Soviet economy, which could never cope with its difficulties on its own, is continually getting material and technological assistance. The major construction projects in the initial five-year plan were built exclusively with American technology and materials. Even Stalin recognized that two thirds of what was needed was obtained from the West. And if today the Soviet Union has powerful military and police forces—in a country which is poor by contemporary standards—forces which are used to crush our movement for freedom in the Soviet Union—we have Western capital to thank for this as well.

Let me remind you of a recent incident which some of you may have read about in the newspapers, although others might have missed it: certain of your businessmen, on their own initiative, set up an exhibit of criminological technology in Moscow. This was the most recent and elaborate technology that here, in your country, is used to catch criminals, to bug them, to spy on them, to photograph them, to tail them, to identify them. It was all put on exhibit in Moscow in order that the Soviet KGB agents could study it, as if the businessmen did not understand what sort of criminals would be hunted down by the KGB.

The Soviet government was extremely interested in this technology and decided to purchase it. And your businessmen were quite willing to sell it. Only when a few sober voices here raised an uproar against it was this deal blocked. But you must realize how clever the KGB is. This technology didn't have to stay two or three weeks in a Soviet building under Soviet guard. Two or three nights were enough for the KGB to examine and copy it. And if today persons are being hunted down by the best and most advanced technology, for this I can also thank your Western capitalists.

This is something which is almost incomprehensible to the human mind: a burning greed for profit that goes beyond all reason, all self-control, all conscience, only to get money.

I must say that Lenin predicted this whole process. Lenin, who spent most of his life in the West and not in Russia, who knew the West much better than Russia, always wrote and said that the Western capitalists would do anything to strengthen the economy of the U.S.S.R. They will compete with each other to sell us cheaper goods and sell them quicker, so that the Soviets will buy from one rather than from the other. He said: They will bring us everything themselves without thinking about their future. And, in a difficult moment, at a party meeting in Moscow, he said: "Comrades, don't panic, when things get very tough for us, we will give the bourgeoisie a rope, and the bourgeoisie will hang itself."

Then Karl Radek, who was a very resourceful wit, said: "Vladimir Ilyich, but where are we going to get enough rope to hang the whole bourgeoisie?"

Lenin effortlessly replied, "They will sell it to us themselves."

For decades on end, throughout the 1920's, the 1930's, the 1940's, and 1950's, the Soviet press kept writing: Western capitalism, your end is near. We will destroy you.

But it was as if the capitalists had not heard, could not understand, could not believe this.

Nikita Khrushchev came here and said, "We will bury you!" They didn't believe that either. They took it as a joke.

Now, of course, they have become more clever in our country. Today they don't say "We are going to bury you," now they say "Détente."

Nothing has changed in Communist ideology. The goals are the same as they were, but instead of the artless Khrushchev, who couldn't hold his tongue, now they say "Détente."

In order to make this clear, I will take the liberty of presenting a short historic survey—the history of these relations which in different periods have been called "trade," "stabilization of the situation," "recognition of realities," and now "détente." These relations have at least a forty-year history.

Let me remind you with *what kind* of system relations began.

The system was installed by an armed uprising.

It dispersed the Constituent Assembly.

It capitulated to Germany—the common enemy.

It introduced punishment and execution without trial through the Cheka.

It crushed workers' strikes.

It plundered the countryside to such an unbelievable extent that the peasants revolted, and when this happened it crushed the peasants in the bloodiest possible manner.

It smashed the Church.

It reduced twenty provinces of our country to utter famine.

This was in 1921, the infamous Volga famine. It was a typical Communist technique: to struggle for power without thinking of the fact that the productivity is collapsing, that the fields are not being sown, that the factories stand idle, that the country is sinking into poverty and famine—but when poverty and hunger do come, then to turn to the humanitarian world for help. We see this in North Vietnam today, Portugal is on the same path. And the same thing happened in Russia in 1921. When the three-year civil war, started by the Communists —and "civil war" was a slogan of the Communists, civil war was Lenin's purpose; read Lenin, this was his aim and his slogan—when they had ruined Russia by civil war, then they asked America, "America, feed our hungry." And indeed, generous and magnanimous America did feed our hungry.

The so-called American Relief Administration was set up, headed by your future President Hoover, and indeed many millions of Russian lives were saved by this organization of yours.

But what sort of gratitude did you receive for this? In the U.S.S.R. not only did they try to erase this whole event from the popular memory—it's almost impossible in the Soviet press today to find any reference to the American Relief Administration—they even denounced it as a clever spy organization, a cunning scheme of American imperialism to set up a spy network in Russia.

I continue: this was a system that introduced the first concentration camps in the history of the world.

This was a system that, in the twentieth century, was the first to introduce the use of hostages—that is to say, to seize not the person whom they were seeking, but rather a member of his family or simply someone at random, and to shoot him.

Such a system of hostages and the persecution of families exists to this day. It is still the most powerful weapon of persecution, because the bravest person, who is not afraid for himself, can flinch at a threat to his family.

This was a system which was the first—long before Hitler—to employ false announcements of registration, that is to say: "Such and such persons must appear to register." People would comply and then they were taken away to be killed. For technical reasons we didn't have gas chambers in those days. We used barges. A hundred or a thousand persons were put into a barge and then it was sunk.

This was a system which deceived the workers in all of its decrees—the decree on land, the decree on peace, the decree on factories, the decree on freedom of the press.

This was a system which exterminated all other parties. And let me make it clear to you that it not only disbanded each party, but destroyed its members. All members of every non-Communist party were exterminated.

This was a system which carried out genocide of the peasantry. Fifteen million peasants were shipped off to their deaths.

This was a system which introduced serfdom, the so-called passport system.

This was a system which, in time of peace, artificially created a famine, causing six million persons to die in the Ukraine between 1932 and 1933. They died on the very threshold of Europe. And Europe didn't even notice it. The world didn't even notice it. Six million persons!

I could continue this enumeration, but I must

stop because I have come to the year 1933 when, after all the facts I have named, your President Roosevelt and your Congress decided that this system was worthy of diplomatic recognition, of friendship, and of assistance.

Let me remind you that the great Washington did not agree to recognize the French Convention because of its savagery. Let me remind you that in 1933 voices were raised in your country objecting to recognition of the Soviet Union. However, this recognition took place and it was the beginning of friendship and ultimately of a military alliance.

Let us recall that in 1904 the American press was delighted at the Japanese victories and everyone wanted Russia's defeat because it was a conservative country. And in 1914 reproaches were directed at France and England for having entered into an alliance with such a conservative country as Russia.

The scope and the direction of my speech today do not permit me to say more about pre-revolutionary Russia. I will only note that information about pre-revolutionary Russia was obtained by the West from persons who were either not sufficiently competent or not sufficiently scrupulous. I will cite for the sake of comparison some figures which you can read for yourself in *The Gulag Archipelago*, which has already been published in the United States, and perhaps many of you may have read it. Here are the figures:

According to the calculations of specialists, based on the most precise and objective statistics, in the eighty years that preceded the Revolution in Russia—years of revolutionary activity with attempts on the Tsar's life, the assassination of a Tsar, revolutionary uprisings—during these years an average of seventeen persons a year were executed. The notorious Spanish Inquisition, during the decades when it was at the height of its murderous activity, executed perhaps ten persons a month. In *The Gulag Archipelago* I cite a book which was published by the Cheka in 1920, proudly reporting on its revolutionary achievements in 1918 and 1919 and apologizing that its data were not quite complete: in 1918 and 1919 the Cheka executed, without trial, more than a thousand persons a month! This was written by the Cheka itself, before it understood how this would appear in historical perspective.

In 1937–8, at the height of Stalin's terror, if we divide the number of persons executed by the number of months, we get more than forty thousand persons shot per month! Here are the figures: seventeen a year, ten a month, more than one thousand a month, more than forty thousand a month! Thus, that which had made it difficult for the democratic West to form an alliance with pre-revolutionary Russia had, by 1941, grown to such an extent, yet still did not prevent the entire united democracies of the world—England, France, the United States, Canada, Australia, and other small countries—from entering into a military alliance with the Soviet Union. How is this to be explained? How can we understand it?

Here we can offer a few explanations. The first, I think, is that the entire united democracies of the world were too weak to fight against Hitler's Germany. If this is the case, then it is a terrible sign. It is a terrifying portent for the present day. If all these countries together could not defeat Hitler's little Germany, what are they going to do today, when more than half the globe is inundated by totalitarianism? I don't want to accept this explanation.

The second explanation is that perhaps there was simply panic among the statesmen of the day. They simply didn't have sufficient confidence in themselves, they had no strength of spirit, and in this confused state they decided to enter into an alliance with Soviet totalitarianism. But this is also not flattering to the West.

Finally, the third explanation is that it was a deliberate choice. Democracy did not wish to defend itself. For defense it wanted to make use of another totalitarian system, the Soviet totalitarian system. I'm not talking now about the moral worth of such a choice, I'm going to talk about that later. But in terms of simple calculation, how shortsighted it is, what profound self-deception it demonstrates!

We have a Russian proverb: "Don't call a wolf to help you against the dogs." If dogs are attacking and tearing at you, fight against the dogs; do not call a wolf for help. Because when the wolves come, they will destroy the dogs or drive them away, but they will tear you apart as well.

World democracy could have defeated one totalitarian regime after another, the German, then the Soviet. Instead, it strengthened Soviet totalitarianism, consented to the birth of a third totalitarianism, that of China, and all this finally precipitated the present world situation.

Roosevelt, in Teheran, during one of his last toasts, said the following: "I do not doubt that the three of us"—meaning Roosevelt, Churchill, and

Stalin—"are leading our peoples in accordance with their desires and their aims." How can this be understood? Let the historians worry about that. At the time, we listened and were astonished. We thought, "When we reach Europe, we will meet the Americans, and we will tell them." I was among the troops that were marching toward the Elbe. A little bit farther and I would have reached it and would have shaken the hands of your American soldiers. But just before that happened, I was taken off to prison and my meeting did not take place.

But now, after a great delay, the same hand has thrown me out of the country and here I am. After a delay of thirty years, my Elbe is here, today. I have come to tell you, as a friend of the United States, what, as friends, we wanted to tell you then, but what our soldiers were also prevented from telling you on the Elbe.

There is another Russian proverb: "The yes-man is your enemy, but your friend will argue with you." It is precisely because I am the friend of the United States, precisely because my speech is prompted by friendship, that I have come to tell you: "My friends, I'm not going to give you sugary words. The situation in the world is not just dangerous, it isn't just threatening, it is catastrophic."

Something that is incomprehensible to the ordinary human mind has taken place. In any case, the powerless, average Soviet people could not understand, year after year and decade after decade, what was happening. How were we to explain it? England, France, the United States, were the victors in World War II. Victorious states always dictate peace: they create the sort of situation which conforms to their philosophy, their concept of liberty, their concept of national interest. Instead of this, beginning in Yalta, your Western statesmen for some inexplicable reason signed one capitulation after another. Never did the West or your President Roosevelt impose any conditions on the Soviet Union for obtaining aid. He gave unlimited aid, and then unlimited concessions. Without any necessity whatever, the occupation of Mongolia, Moldavia, Estonia, Latvia, Lithuania was silently recognized in Yalta. After that, almost nothing was done to protect Eastern Europe, and seven or eight more countries were surrendered.

Stalin demanded that the Soviet citizens who did not want to return home be handed over to him, and the Western countries handed over 1.5 million human beings. How was this done? They were taken by force. English soldiers killed Russians who did not want to become prisoners of Stalin, and drove them by force to Stalin to be exterminated. This has recently come to light, just a few years ago. A million and a half human beings. How could the Western democracies have done this?

After that, for another thirty years, the constant retreat, the surrender of one country after another, to such a point that there are Soviet satellites even in Africa, almost all of Asia is taken over by them, Portugal is rolling down the precipice.

During those thirty years, more was surrendered to totalitarianism than any defeated country has ever surrendered after any war in history. There was no war, but there might as well have been.

For a long time we in the East couldn't understand this. We couldn't understand the flabbiness of the truce concluded in Vietnam. Any average Soviet citizen understood that this was a sly device which made it possible for North Vietnam to take over South Vietnam when it so chose. And then this arrangement was rewarded by the Nobel Prize for Peace—a tragic and ironic prize.

A very dangerous state of mind can arise as a result of these thirty years of retreat: give in as quickly as possible, give up as quickly as possible, peace and quiet at any cost.

This is what many Western papers wrote: "Let's hurry up and end the bloodshed in Vietnam and have national unity." (But at the Berlin Wall no one talks of national unity.) One of your leading newspapers, after the fall of Vietnam, had a full headline: THE BLESSED SILENCE. I would not wish that kind of "blessed silence" on my worst enemy. I would not wish that kind of national unity on my worst enemy.

I spent eleven years in the Gulag Archipelago, and for half of my lifetime I have studied this question. Looking at this terrible tragedy in Vietnam from a distance, I can tell you that a million persons will simply be exterminated, while four to five million (in accordance with the scale of Vietnam) will find themselves in concentration camps and will be used to rebuild Vietnam. And you already know what is happening in Cambodia. It is a case of genocide. Full and complete destruction, only in a new form. Once again their technology is not up to building gas chambers. So, in a few hours, the entire capital city—the guilty capital city—is emptied out: old people, women, children are driven out without belongings, without food. "Go and die!"

It is very dangerous for one's view of the world when this feeling comes on: "Go ahead, give it up."

We already hear voices in your country and in the West: "Give up Korea and let's live quietly." Give up Portugal, of course; give up Japan, give up Israel, give up Taiwan, the Philippines, Malaysia, Thailand, give up ten more African countries. Just let us live in peace and quiet. Let us drive our big cars on our splendid highways; let us play tennis and golf unperturbed; let us mix our cocktails as we are accustomed to doing; let us see the beautiful smile and a glass of wine on every page of our magazines.

But look how things have turned out: in the West this has all turned into an accusation against the United States. We hear many voices saying, "It's your fault, America." I must today decisively defend the United States against these accusations.

I must say that the United States, of all the countries of the West, is the least guilty and has done the most in order to prevent it. The United States has helped Europe to win the First and the Second World Wars. It twice raised Europe from postwar destruction—twice—for ten, twenty, thirty years it has stood as a shield protecting Europe while European countries counted their nickels to avoid paying for their armies (better yet, to have none at all), to avoid paying for armaments, thinking about how to leave NATO, knowing that in any case America will protect them. These countries started it all, despite their thousand-year-old civilization and culture, even though they are closer to the danger and should have seen it more clearly.

I came to your continent; for two months I have been traveling in its wide-open spaces and I agree: here you must make an effort to understand the acuteness of the world situation. The United States has long shown itself to be the most magnanimous, the most generous country in the world. Wherever there is a flood, an earthquake, a fire, a natural disaster, an epidemic, who is the first to help? The United States. Who helps the most and unselfishly? The United States.

And what do we hear in reply? Reproaches, curses, "Yankee Go Home." American cultural centers are burned, and representatives from the Third World jump on tables to vote against the United States at the U.N.

But none of this takes the load off America's shoulders. Whether you like it or not, the course of history has made you the leaders of the world. Your country can no longer think provincially. Your political leaders can no longer think only of their own states, of their own parties, of petty situations, which may or may not contribute to success at election time. You must think about the whole world. When a new political crisis arises (I believe we have just come to the end of a very acute crisis and the next one might come at any moment), the main decisions will fall inevitably on the shoulders of the United States.

In my stay here, I have heard some explanations of the situation. Let me quote some of them: "It is impossible to protect those who do not have the will to defend themselves." I agree with that, but this was said about South Vietnam. Yet in one half of today's Europe and in three quarters of today's world the will for self-defense is even less than it was in South Vietnam.

We are told: "We cannot defend those who are unable to defend themselves with their own human resources." But against the overwhelming forces of totalitarianism, when all of this power is thrown against a country—no country can defend itself with its own resources. For instance, Japan doesn't have a standing army.

We are told: "We should not protect those who do not have a full democracy." This is the most remarkable argument of all. This is the leitmotif I hear in your newspapers and in the speeches of some of your political leaders. Who in the world, when on the front line of defense against totalitarianism, has ever been able to sustain a full democracy? You, the united democracies of the world, were not able to sustain it. America, England, France, Canada, Australia together did not sustain it. At the first threat of Hitlerism, you stretched out your hands to Stalin. You call that sustaining democracy? Hardly.

And there are other arguments (there have been a great many such speeches): "If the Soviet Union is going to use détente for its own ends, then we . . ." But what will happen then? The Soviet Union has used détente, is using it now, and will continue to use it in its own interests! For example, China and the Soviet Union, both actively participating in détente, have quietly grabbed three countries of Indochina. True, perhaps as a consolation, China will send you a ping-pong team. Just as the Soviet Union once sent you the pilots who crossed the North Pole. And in a few days there will be the flight into space together.

A typically well-staged diversion. I remember very well the time, June 1937, when Chkalov, Baidukov, and Belyakov heroically flew over the North Pole and landed in the state of Washington. This was the very year when Stalin was executing more than forty thousand persons a month. And Stalin knew what he was doing. He sent those pilots and aroused in you a naïve delight—the friendship of two countries across the North Pole. The pilots were heroes, nobody will deny them that. But this was a show to divert you from the real events of 1937. And what is the occasion now? Could it be an anniversary of that flight thirty-eight years ago? Is thirty-eight years some kind of an anniversary? No, it is simply necessary to cover up Vietnam. Once again, those pilots were sent here. The Chkalov Memorial was unveiled in the state of Washington. Chkalov was a hero and is worthy of a memorial. But to present the true picture, there should have been a wall behind the memorial and on it there should have been a bas-relief showing the executions, showing the skulls and skeletons.

We are also told (I apologize for so many quotes, but there are many more in your press and radio): "We cannot ignore the fact that North Vietnam and the Khmer Rouge have violated the agreement, but we're ready to look to the future." What does this mean? It means: let them exterminate people. If these murderers, who live by violence, these executioners, offer us détente, we will be happy to go along with them. As Willy Brandt once said: "I

would even be willing to have détente with Stalin."
At a time when Stalin was executing forty thousand
a month he would have been willing to have détente
with Stalin?

Look into the future! This is how they looked
into the future in 1933 and 1941, but it was a shortsighted look. This is how they looked into the future
two years ago when a senseless, incomprehensible,
non-guaranteed truce in Vietnam was negotiated.
Once again it was a shortsighted view. There was
such a hurry to make this truce that they forgot to
liberate your own Americans from captivity. They
were in such a hurry to sign this document that
some three thousand Americans were left there:
"Well, they have vanished; we can get by without
them." How was this done? How can this be? Part
of them, indeed, may be missing in action, but the
leaders of North Vietnam themselves have admitted
that some of them are still being kept in prison.
And do they return your countrymen? No, instead
of returning them, they keep laying down new conditions. At first they said, "Remove Thieu from
power." Now they say, "Let the United States re-
store a unified Vietnam, otherwise it's very difficult
to find these people."

If the government of North Vietnam has difficulty

explaining to you what happened to your brothers, your American POW's who have not yet returned, I can explain this quite clearly on the basis of my experience in the Gulag Archipelago. There is a law in the Archipelago that those who have been treated the most harshly and who have withstood the most bravely, who are the most honest, the most courageous, the most unbending, never again come out into the world. They are never again shown to the world because they will tell tales that the human mind can barely accept. Some of your returned POW's told you that they were tortured. This means that those who have remained were tortured even more, but did not yield an inch. These are your best people. These are your foremost heroes, who, in a solitary combat, have stood the test. And today, unfortunately, they cannot take courage from our applause. They can't hear it from their solitary cells where they may either die or remain for thirty years like Raoul Wallenberg, the Swedish diplomat who was seized in 1945 in the Soviet Union. He has been imprisoned for thirty years and they will not give him up.

And yet you had some hysterical public figures who said: "I will go to North Vietnam. I will get on my knees and beg them to release our prisoners of war." This is no longer a political act—this is masochism.

To make you understand properly what détente has meant in these forty years—friendships, stabilization of the situation, trade, etc.—I must tell you something which you have not seen or heard: how it looked from the other side. Let me give you some examples. Mere acquaintance with an American, and God forbid that you should sit with him in a café or restaurant, meant a ten-year term for suspicion of espionage.

In the first volume of *The Gulag Archipelago* I tell of an event which was recounted not by some insignificant arrested person but by all of the members of the Supreme Court of the U.S.S.R. during that brief period when I was in the good graces of the regime under Khrushchev. A Soviet citizen had been in the United States and on his return said that they have wonderful roads there. The KGB arrested him and demanded a term of ten years, but the judge said: "I don't object, but there is not enough evidence. Couldn't you find something else against him?" So the judge was exiled to Sakhalin because he dared to argue, and they gave the other man ten years. Just imagine what "lie" he had told! And what "praise" this was of American imperialism: in America there are good roads! Ten years.

In 1945–6 many persons passed through our prison cells. They had not cooperated with Hitler, although there were some of those too. As a rule they were not guilty of anything, but simply had been in the West and had been liberated from German prison camps by the Americans. This was considered a criminal act: liberated by the Americans. It meant he has seen the good life. If he comes back he will talk about it. The most terrible thing is not what he did but what he would talk about. And all such persons got ten-year terms.

During Nixon's last visit to Moscow your American correspondents gave their reports from the streets of Moscow: Here I am, going down a Russian street with a microphone and asking ordinary Soviet citizens: "Tell me, please, what do you think of the meeting between Nixon and Brezhnev?" And, amazingly, every last person answered: "Wonderful. I'm delighted. I'm absolutely overjoyed!"

What does this mean? If I'm going down a street in Moscow and some American comes up to me with a microphone and asks me something, then I know for certain that a member of the state security is close by, also with a microphone, and is recording everything I say. Do you think that I'm going to say something that is going to put me in prison immediately? Of course I say "It's wonderful, I'm overjoyed."

But what is the worth of such correspondents if they simply transfer Western methods over there without thinking things through?

For many years you helped us with Lend-Lease, but we've now done everything to forget this, to erase it from our minds, not to recall it if at all possible. Before I came here, I delayed my visit to Washington a little in order to take a look at some ordinary parts of America, to visit several states and simply to talk with people. I was told, and I learned this for the first time, that in every state during the war years there were Soviet-American friendship societies which collected assistance for the Soviet people—warm clothes, canned food, gifts—and sent them to the Soviet Union. Not only did we never see these things or receive them (they were distributed somewhere among the privileged circles), but no one even told us that this was being done. I only learned about it for the first time here, this month, in the United States.

Everything poisonous which could be said about

the United States was said in Stalin's day. And all of this is a heavy sediment which can be stirred up at any time. Any day the newspapers can come out with the headline BLOODTHIRSTY AMERICAN IMPERIALISM WANTS TO SEIZE CONTROL OF THE WORLD, and this poison will rise up again and many people in our country will believe and will consider you aggressors. This is how détente has been managed on our side.

The Soviet system is so closed that it is almost impossible for you to understand it from here. Your theoreticians and scholars write monographs, they try to understand and explain what is taking place there. Here are some of these naïve explanations, which cannot fail to amuse us Soviet people. It is said, for example, that the Soviet leaders have now given up their inhumane ideology. Not at all. They haven't given it up one bit. Others say that in the Kremlin there are some on the left, some on the right; they are fighting with each other, and we have to behave in such a way so that we don't interfere with those on the left. This is all fantasy: left, right. There is some sort of a struggle for power, of course, but they all agree on the essentials.

There also exists the following theory: that now, thanks to the growth of technology, there is a technocracy in the Soviet Union, a growing number of engineers, and the engineers are now running the economy and they, not the party, will soon determine the fate of the country. But I will tell you that the engineers will determine the fate of the country just as much as our generals will determine the fate of the army. That means zero. Everything is done the way the party demands. That is our system. Judge it for yourself.

It is a system where for forty years there have not been genuine elections, but simply a comedy, a farce. Thus, a system which has no legislative machinery. It is a system without an independent press; a system without an independent judiciary; where the people have no influence either on external or internal policy; where any thought which is different from the state's is crushed.

And let me tell you that electronic bugging in our country is such a simple thing that it is a matter of everyday life. You had an incident in the United States where a bugging caused an uproar which lasted for a year and a half. For us it's an everyday matter. Almost every apartment, every institution has its bug, and it doesn't surprise us in the least —we are used to it.

It is a system where unmasked butchers of

millions, like Molotov and some lesser men, have never been tried in the courts but retire on enormous pensions in the greatest comfort. It is a system where the show still goes on today and where every foreigner who wants to see the country is surrounded by several planted agents working according to a fixed scenario. It is a system where the constitution has never been adhered to for one single day; where all the decisions are reached in secrecy, among a small, irresponsible clique and are then flung down on us and on you like a bolt of lightning.

And what are the signatures of these people worth? How could one rely on their signatures in the documents of détente? You might ask your specialists now and they'll tell you that in recent years the Soviet Union has succeeded in achieving superiority in chemical weapons and in missiles over the United States.

So what are we to conclude from that? Is détente needed or not? Not only is it needed, it is as necessary as air. It is the only way of saving the earth —instead of a world war to create détente, a true détente, and if it has already been ruined by the bad word which we use for it—"détente"—then we should find another word.

I would say that there are very few, only three, main characteristics of such a true détente.

In the first place, there would be disarmament —but a dismantling of the weapons of war as well as those of violence. We must stop using not only the kind of arms that are used to destroy one's neighbors but also the kind that are used to oppress one's fellow countrymen. It is hardly détente if we here can spend our time agreeably, while over there people are groaning and dying or confined in psychiatric hospitals. Doctors are making their evening rounds, injecting people with the third daily dose of drugs which destroy the brain.

The second sign of true détente, I would say, is the following: that it not be based on smiles, not on verbal concessions, but on a firm foundation. You know the words from the Bible: Build not on sand, but on rock. There has to be a guarantee that détente will not be violated overnight. For this the other party to the agreement must have its acts subject to control by public opinion, by the press, and by a freely elected parliament. And until such control exists there is absolutely no guarantee.

There is a third simple condition. What kind of détente is it when they employ the sort of malevolent propaganda which is proudly called "ideological warfare" in the Soviet Union? Let us not have that. If we're going to be friends, let's be friends; if we're going to have détente, then let's have détente, and an end to ideological warfare.

The Soviet Union and the Communist countries know how to conduct negotiations. For a long time they make no concessions and then they give in just a little bit. Right away there is rejoicing: "Look, they've made a concession; it's time to sign." For two years the European negotiators of thirty-five countries have painfully been negotiating and their nerves have been stretched to the breaking point; finally they gave in. A few women from the Communist countries may now marry foreigners. A few newspapermen will now be permitted to travel a little more than before. They give one one-thousandth of what natural law should provide—things which people should be able to do even before such negotiations are undertaken—and already there is joy. And here in the West we hear many voices that say: "Look, they're making concessions; it's time to sign."

During these two years of negotiations, in all the countries of Eastern Europe, even in Yugoslavia and Romania, the pressure has increased, the oppression intensified. And it is precisely now that the Austrian chancellor says, "We must sign this agreement as rapidly as possible."

What sort of an agreement will this be? The proposed agreement is the funeral of Eastern Europe. It means that Western Europe will finally, once and for all, sign away Eastern Europe, stating that it is perfectly willing to see Eastern Europe oppressed, only please don't bother us. And the Austrian chancellor thinks that if all these countries are pushed into a mass grave, Austria, at the very edge, will somehow survive and not fall into it as well.

And we, from the whole of our life experience there, have concluded that there is only one way to withstand violence: with firmness.

You have to understand the nature of Communism. The very ideology of Communism, all of Lenin's teachings, are that anyone who doesn't take what's lying in front of him is considered a fool. If you can take it, do so. If you can attack, strike. But if there's a wall, then retreat. The Communist leaders respect only firmness and have contempt for persons who continually give in to them. Your people are now saying—and this is the last quotation I am going to give you from the statements of your leaders—"Power, without any at-

tempt at conciliation, will lead to a world conflict."
But I would say that power with continual ac-
quiescence is not power at all.

From our experience I can tell you that only
firmness makes it possible to withstand the assaults
of Communist totalitarianism. History offers many
examples, and let me give you some of them. Look
at little Finland in 1939, which by its own forces
withstood the attack. You, in 1948, defended Berlin
only by your firmness of spirit, and there was no
world conflict. In Korea in 1950 you stood up to
the Communists, only by your firmness, and there
was no world conflict. In 1962 you forced the
missiles to be removed from Cuba. Again it was
only firmness, and there was no world conflict. The
late Konrad Adenauer conducted firm negotiations
with Khrushchev and initiated a genuine détente
with Khrushchev, who started to make concessions.
If he hadn't been removed, he would have gone to
Germany that winter to continue the genuine
détente.

Let me remind you of the weakness of a man
whose name is rarely associated with weakness—
Lenin. When he came to power, Lenin, panic-
stricken, gave up to Germany everything Germany
demanded. Whatever they asked for. Germany took

as much as it wanted and said, "Give Armenia to Turkey." And Lenin said, "Fine." It's almost an unknown fact that Lenin petitioned the Kaiser to act as intermediary to persuade the Ukraine to settle a boundary between the Communists and the Ukraine. It wasn't a question of seizing the Ukraine but only of creating this boundary.

We, the dissidents of the U.S.S.R., have no tanks, no weapons, no organization. We have nothing. Our hands are empty. We have only our hearts and what we have lived through in the half century under this system. And whenever we have found the firmness within ourselves to stand up for our rights, we have done so. It is only by firmness of spirit that we have withstood. And if I am standing here before you, it is not because of the kindness or the good will of Communism, not thanks to détente, but due to my own firmness and your firm support. They knew that I would not yield an inch, not a hair's breadth. And when they could do nothing they themselves fell back.

This is not easy. We learned from the difficulties of our own life. And if you yourselves—any one of you—were in the same difficult situation, you would have learned the same thing. Take Vladimir Bukovsky, whose name is now almost forgotten. I don't want to enumerate a lot of names because however many I might mention there are still more, and when we resolve the question with two or three names it is as if we forget and betray the others. Instead, we should remember figures: there are tens of thousands of political prisoners in our country and—by the calculation of British specialists— seven thousand persons are now under compulsory psychiatric treatment. For example, Vladimir Bukovsky. It was proposed to him, "All right, we'll free you. Go to the West and shut up." And this young man, a youth now on the verge of death, said: "No, I won't go under those conditions. I have written about the persons you have put in insane asylums. You release them and then I'll go to the West." This is what I mean by that firmness of spirit to stand up against granite and tanks.

Finally, to evaluate everything that I have said to you, we need not remain on the level of practical calculations. Why did such and such a country act in such and such a way? What were they counting on? Instead, we should rise above this to the moral level and say: "In 1933 and in 1941 your leaders and the whole Western world made an unprincipled deal with totalitarianism." We will have to pay for this; someday it will come back to haunt us. For thirty years we have been paying for it. And we're going to pay for it in an even worse way in the future.

One cannot think only on the low level of political calculations. It is also necessary to think of what is noble, and what is honorable—not just of what is profitable. Resourceful Western legal scholars have now introduced the term "legal realism," which they can use to obscure any moral evaluation of affairs. They say, "Recognize realities: if certain laws have been established in countries ruled by violence, these laws still must be recognized and respected."

At the present time it is widely accepted among lawyers that law is higher than morality—law is something which is shaped and developed, whereas morality is something inchoate and amorphous. This is not the case. The opposite is true: morality is higher than law! Law is our human attempt to embody in rules a part of that moral sphere which is above us. We try to understand this morality, bring it down to earth, and present it in the form of law. Sometimes we are more successful, sometimes less. Sometimes we have a mere caricature of morality, but morality is always higher than law. This view must never be abandoned. We must acknowledge it with our hearts and souls.

In the twentieth century it is almost a joke in the Western world to use words like "good" and "evil." They have become old-fashioned concepts, yet they are very real and genuine. These are concepts from a sphere which is above us. And instead of getting involved in base, petty, shortsighted political calculations and games we must recognize that a concentration of evil and a tremendous force of hatred is spreading throughout the world. We must stand up against it and not hasten to give, give, give, everything that it wants to swallow.

Today there are two major trends in the world. The first is the one I have just described to you, which has been going on for more than thirty years. It is a process of shortsighted concessions; a process of giving up and giving up and giving up in the hope that perhaps at some point the wolf will have eaten enough.

The second trend is one which I consider the key to everything and which, I predict, will bring all of us our future. Under the cast-iron shell of Communism—for twenty years in the Soviet Union and

for a shorter time in other Communist countries—
a liberation of the human spirit is occurring. New
generations are growing up, steadfast in their struggle with evil, unwilling to accept unprincipled com-
promises, preferring to lose everything—salary, living conditions, life itself—so as not to sacrifice
conscience, unwilling to make deals with evil.

This trend has gone so far that, in the Soviet
Union today, Marxism has fallen to such a low point
that it has become a joke, an object of contempt.
No serious person in our country today, not even
university and high-school students, can talk about
Marxism without a smile or a sneer. But this process
of our liberation, which obviously will entail social
transformations, is slower than the first one—the
process of concessions. Over there, when we see
these concessions we cannot understand. Why so
quickly? Why so precipitously? Why yield several
countries in one year?

I started by saying that you are the allies of our
liberation movement in the Communist countries.
I call upon you: let us think together and try to see
how we can adjust the relationship between these
two trends. Whenever you help the persons persecuted in the Soviet Union, you not only display

magnanimity and nobility, you are not only defending them, but yourselves as well. You are defending your own future.

So let us try and see how far we can go to stop this senseless and immoral process of endless concessions to the aggressor, these slick legal arguments for giving up one country after another. Why must we hand over to Communist totalitarianism more and more technology—complex, sophisticated technology which it needs for armaments and for oppressing its own citizens? If we can at least slow down that process of concession, if not stop it altogether, and make it possible for the process of liberation to continue in the Communist countries, then ultimately these two processes will yield us our future.

On our crowded planet there are no longer any "internal affairs." The Communist leaders say, "Don't interfere in our internal affairs. Let us strangle our citizens in peace and quiet." But I tell you: Interfere more and more. Interfere as much as you can. We beg you to come and interfere.

Understanding my own task in the same way, I have perhaps interfered today in your internal affairs, or at least touched upon them, and I apologize for it.

I have traveled around the United States and this

has been added to my earlier understanding of it—
what I have heard from listening to the radio, from
talking to men of experience.

For me and my friends, for people who think the
way I do over there, for all ordinary Soviet citizens,
America evokes a mixture of admiration and com-
passion. Admiration for your own tremendous
forces which perhaps you don't even recognize yourselves. You're a country of the future, a young
country, with yet untapped possibilities, enormous
territory, great breadth of spirit, generosity, magnanimity. But these qualities—strength, generosity,
and magnanimity—are usually combined in a man
and even in a whole country with trustfulness. And
this has already done you a disservice several times.

I would like to call upon America to be more
careful with its trust to prevent those pundits who
are attempting to establish fine degrees of justice
and even finer legal shades of equality (some because of their distorted outlook, others because of
shortsightedness, still others out of self-interest), to
prevent them from using the struggle for peace and
for social justice to lead you down a false road.
They are trying to weaken you; they are trying to
disarm your strong and magnificent country in the
face of this fearful threat—one which has never

before been seen in the history of the world. Not only in the history of your country, but in the history of the world.

I call upon you: Ordinary working men of America, represented here by your trade-union movement, do not let yourselves become weak. Do not let yourselves be led in the wrong direction. Let us try to slow down the process of concessions and help the process of liberation!

May I express our deep appreciation to Alexander Solzhenitsyn for his inspiring address, for the thoughts that he left with us at a time when, God knows, the world needs to think more about human freedom. The world needs to think more about those who are losing their freedom every day.

America must, in my opinion, shape up to this challenge as the leader of the free world, because if America doesn't lead the free world, the free world, I'm afraid, has no leader. GEORGE MEANY

[50]

[*JULY* 9, 1975]

Introduction by Lane Kirkland

A principle of mechanics tells us that, given a long-enough lever, one man can move the entire world. Alexander Solzhenitsyn is a living test of that principle.

His lever is his pen, extended far beyond his reach by his mind, his talent, his courage, and his unshakable integrity.

He seeks to move a world that today seems far gone in madness and in cowardice. A world where terror, murder, and oppression are welcomed and are exalted in the glass and marble temples of universal peace and justice that were built by a highly optimistic generation after World War II.

He stands as a living, monumental reproach to

*all of those statesmen and leaders who today raise
the practice of abstention on basic moral issues
to the level of high national policy and who flee
from any test of the good will, the graces, and
the kindly disposition of the most deadly enemies
of mankind.*

*His work is not devoted to the advancement of
any political doctrine or fashion in political dis-
course or any passing notion of expediency—but
to the most elemental values of human dignity,
human justice, and human freedom.*

*The AFL-CIO is proud and honored to stand
with him in that cause. I am privileged now to
introduce Alexander Solzhenitsyn.*

I s it possible or impossible to transmit the experience of those who have suffered to those who
have yet to suffer? Can one part of humanity learn
from the bitter experience of another or can it not?
Is it possible or impossible to warn someone of
danger?

How many witnesses have been sent to the West

Mr. Solzhenitsyn delivered this speech in New York City at a
luncheon which was given in his honor by the AFL-CIO and
hosted by Lane Kirkland, the union's secretary-treasurer.

in the last sixty years? How many waves of immigrants? How many millions of persons? They are all here. You meet them every day. You know who they are: if not by their spiritual disorientation, their grief, their melancholy, then you can distinguish them by their accents or their external appearance. Coming from different countries, without consulting with one another, they have brought out exactly the same experience; they tell you exactly the same thing: they warn you of what is now taking place and, of what has taken place in the past. But the proud skyscrapers stand on, jut into the sky, and say: It will never happen here. This will never come to us. It is not possible here.

It can happen. It is possible. As a Russian proverb says: "When it happens to you, you'll know it's true."

But do we really have to wait for the moment when the knife is at our throat? Couldn't it be possible, ahead of time, to assess soberly the world-wide menace that threatens to swallow the whole world? I was swallowed myself. I have been in the dragon's belly, in its red-hot innards. It was unable to digest me and threw me up. I have come to you as a witness to what it is like there, in the dragon's belly.

It is astonishing that Communism has been writing about itself in the most open way, in black and white, for 125 years, and even more openly, more candidly in the beginning. The *Communist Manifesto,* for instance, which everyone knows by name, and which almost no one ever takes the trouble to read, contains even more terrible things than what has actually been done. It is perfectly amazing. The whole world can read, everyone is literate, yet somehow no one wants to understand. Humanity acts as if it does not understand what Communism is, as if it does not want to understand, is not capable of understanding.

I think it is not only a question of the disguises that Communism has assumed in the last decades. It is rather that the essence of Communism is quite beyond the limits of human understanding. It is hard to believe that people could actually plan such things and carry them out. And it is precisely because its essence is beyond comprehension, perhaps, that Communism is so difficult to understand.

In my last address in Washington I spoke a great deal about the Soviet state system, how it was created and what it is today. But it is perhaps more important to discuss with you the ideology that inspired the system, created it, and still governs it.

It is much more important to understand the essence, and above all the legacy, of this ideology which has not changed at all in 125 years. It has not changed since the day it was created.

That Marxism is not a science is entirely clear to intelligent people in the Soviet Union. One would even feel awkward to refer to it as a science. Leaving aside the exact sciences, such as physics, mathematics, and the natural sciences, even the social sciences can predict an event—when, in what way, and how an event might occur. Communism has never made any such forecasts. It has never said where, when, and precisely what is going to happen. Nothing but declamations. Rhetoric to the effect that the world proletariat will overthrow the world bourgeoisie and the most happy and radiant society will then arise. The fantasies of Marx, Engels, and Lenin break off at this point, not one of them goes any further to describe what this society would be like. They simply said: the most radiant, most happy society. Everything for the sake of man.

I wouldn't want to enumerate for you all the unsuccessful predictions of Marxism, but I can give you a few. For example, it was claimed that the conditions of the working class in the West would deteriorate steadily, get more and more unbearable, until the workers would be reduced to total poverty. (If only in our country we could feed and clothe our working class, provide it with everything, and give it as much leisure as you do!)

Or the famous prediction that Communist revolutions would begin in such advanced industrial countries as England, France, America, Germany. (But it worked out exactly the other way, as you know.) Or the prediction that socialist states would not even exist. As soon as capitalism was overthrown, the state would at once wither away. (Look about you: where can you see states as powerful as in the so-called socialist or Communist countries?) Or the prediction that wars are inherent only to capitalism; as soon as Communism is introduced, all wars will come to an end. (We have also seen enough of this: in Budapest, in Prague, on the Soviet-Chinese border, in the occupation of the Baltic countries, and when Poland was stabbed in the back. We have seen enough of this already, and we will surely see more yet.)

Communism is as crude an attempt to explain society and the individual as if a surgeon were to perform his delicate operations with a meat ax. All that is subtle in human psychology and in the structure of society (which is even more complex), all of this is reduced to crude economic processes. This whole created being—man—is reduced to matter. It is characteristic that Communism is so devoid of arguments that it has none to advance against its opponents in our Communist countries. It lacks arguments and hence there is the club, the prison, the concentration camp, and insane asylums with forced confinement.

Marxism has always opposed freedom. I will quote just a few words from the founding fathers of Communism, Marx and Engels (I quote from the first Soviet edition of 1929): "Reforms are a sign of weakness" (vol. 23, p. 339); "Democracy is more to be feared than monarchy and aristocracy" (vol. 2, p. 369); "Political liberty is a false liberty, worse than the most abject slavery" (vol. 2, p. 394). In their correspondence Marx and Engels frequently stated that terror would be indispensable after achieving power, that "it will be necessary to repeat the year 1793. After achieving power, we'll be considered monsters, but we couldn't care less" (vol. 25, p. 187).

Communism has never concealed the fact that it rejects all absolute concepts of morality. It scoffs at any consideration of "good" and "evil" as indisputable categories. Communism considers morality to be relative, to be a class matter. Depending upon circumstances and the political situation, any act, including murder, even the killing of hundreds of thousands, could be good or could be bad. It all depends upon class ideology. And who defines this ideology? The whole class cannot get together to pass judgment. A handful of people determine what is good and what is bad. But I must say that in this very respect Communism has been most successful. It has infected the whole world with the belief in the relativity of good and evil. Today, many people apart from the Communists are carried away by this idea. Among progressive people, it is considered rather awkward to use seriously such words as "good" and "evil." Communism has managed to persuade all of us that these concepts are old-fashioned and laughable. But if we are to be deprived of the concepts of good and evil, what will be left? Nothing but the manipulation of one another. We will sink to the status of animals.

Both the theory and the practice of Communism are completely inhuman for that reason. There is a word very commonly used these days: "anti-Communism." That is a poor, tasteless locution. It makes it appear as though Communism were something original, fundamental. Therefore, it is taken as the point of departure, and anti-Communism is defined in relation to Communism. I say that this word was poorly selected, that it was put together by people who do not understand etymology. The primary, the eternal concept is humanity, and Communism is anti-humanity. Whoever says "anti-Communism" is saying, in effect, anti-anti-humanity. A poor construction. So we should say: That which is against Communism is for humanity. Not to accept, but to reject this inhuman Communist ideology is simply to be a human being. Such a rejection is more than a political act. It is a protest of our souls against those who would have us forget the concepts of good and evil.

But what is amazing is that apart from all its writings, Communism has offered a multitude of examples for modern man to see. The tanks have rumbled through Budapest. This is nothing. The tanks roar into Czechoslovakia. This is nothing. No one else would have been forgiven, but Communism can be excused. With some kind of strange deliberation, as though God decided to punish them by taking away their reason, the Communists erected the Berlin Wall. It is indeed a monstrous symbol that demonstrates the true meaning of Communism. For fourteen years people have been machine-gunned there, and not only those who wanted to leave the happy Communist society. Recently some foreign boy from the Western side fell into the Spree River. Some people wanted to pull him out, but the East German border guards opened fire. "No, no, don't save him." And so this innocent boy drowned.

Has the Berlin Wall convinced anyone? No again. It is ignored. It's there, but it doesn't affect us: we'll never have a wall like that, and the tanks from Budapest and Prague won't come here either. On all the borders of the Communist countries, the European ones at least, you can find electronic devices for killing anyone who goes across. But people say: "That doesn't threaten us either, we are not afraid of that." In the Communist countries they have developed a system of forced treatment in insane asylums. That's nothing. We're living quietly. Three times a day—right at this very moment—the doctors are making their rounds and injecting substances that destroy the brain. Pay no attention to it. We'll continue to live in peace and quiet here.

There's a certain woman here named Angela Davis. I don't know if you are familiar with her in this country, but in our country, literally, for an entire year, we heard of nothing at all except Angela Davis. There was only Angela Davis in the whole world and she was suffering. We had our ears stuffed with Angela Davis. Little children in school were told to sign petitions in defense of Angela Davis. Little boys and girls, eight and nine years old, were asked to do this. She was set free, as you know. Although she didn't have too difficult a time in this country's jails, she came to recuperate in Soviet resorts. Some Soviet dissidents—but more important, a group of Czech dissidents—addressed an appeal to her: "Comrade Davis, you were in prison. You know how unpleasant it is to sit in prison, especially when you consider yourself innocent. You have such great authority now. Could you help our Czech prisoners? Could you stand up for those people in Czechoslovakia who are being persecuted by the state?" Angela Davis answered: "They deserve what they get. Let them remain in prison." That is the face of Communism. That is the heart of Communism for you.

I would particularly like to remind you today that Communism develops in a straight line and as a single entity, without altering, as people now like to say. Lenin did indeed develop Marxism, but primarily along the lines of ideological intolerance. If you read Lenin, you will be astonished at how much hatred there was in him for the least deviation, whenever some view differed from his even by a hair's breadth. Lenin also developed Marxism in the direction of inhumanity. Before the October Revolution in Russia, Lenin wrote a book called *The Lessons of the Paris Commune*. There he analyzed why the Paris Commune was defeated in 1871. His principal conclusion was that the Commune had not shot, had not killed enough of its enemies. It had destroyed too few people, at a time when it was necessary to kill entire classes and groups. And when he came to power, Lenin did just this.

And then the word "Stalinism" was thought up. This is a term that became very popular. Even in the West they often say now: "If only the Soviet Union doesn't return to Stalinism." But there was never any such thing as Stalinism. It was contrived by Khrushchev and his group in order to blame all the characteristic traits and principal defects of Communism on Stalin—it was a very effective move. But in reality Lenin had managed to give shape to all the main features before Stalin came to power. It is Lenin who deceived the peasants about their land, and the workers about self-management. He is the one who turned the trade unions into organs of oppression. He is the one who created the Cheka, the secret police, and the concentration camps. It is he who sent troops out to the border areas to crush any national movements for liberation and to set up an empire.

The only new thing that Stalin did was based on distrust. When it would have been enough—in order to instill general fear—to jail two people, he arrested a hundred. And those who succeeded Stalin merely returned to the previous tactic: if it is necessary to send two off to jail, then send two, not a hundred. In the eyes of the party, Stalin's entire guilt lay elsewhere: he did not trust his own Communist Party. Due to this alone, the concept of Stalinism was devised. But Stalin had never deviated from the same basic line. They used to sculpt a bas-relief of Marx, Engels, Lenin, and Stalin all together; to this one could add Mao Tse-tung, Kim Il Sung, Ho Chi Minh; they are all in the same line of development.

The following theory is also accepted in the West. It is said that China is a sort of purified, puritanical type of Communism, one which has not degenerated. But China is simply a delayed phase of that so-called War Communism established by Lenin in Russia but which remained in force only until 1921. Lenin established it not at all because the military situation required it but because this is how he envisioned

[63]

the future of their society. But when economic pressure required him to retreat, he introduced the so-called New Economic Policy and he retreated. In China this initial phase has simply lasted longer. China is characterized by all the same traits: massive compulsory labor which is not paid in accordance with its value; work on holidays; forced living in communes; and the incessant dinning of slogans and dogmas that abolish the human essence and deny all individuality to man.

The most frightening aspect of the world Communist system is its unity, its cohesion. Enrico Berlinguer said quite recently that the sun had set on the Comintern. Not at all. It hasn't set. Its energy has been transformed into electricity, which is now pulsing through underground cables. The sun of the Comintern today spreads its energy everywhere in the form of high-voltage electricity. Quite recently there was an incident when Western Communists indignantly denied that Portugal was operating on instructions from Moscow. Of course, Moscow also denied this. And then it was discovered that those very orders had been openly published in the Soviet magazine *Problems of Peace and Socialism*. These were the very instructions that Ponomarev had given. All the apparent differences among the

Communist Parties of the world are imaginary. All are united on one point: your social order must be destroyed.

Why should we be surprised if the world does not understand this? Even the socialists, who are the closest to Communism, do not understand it. They cannot grasp the true nature of Communism. Recently, the leader of the Swedish socialists, Olof Palme, said that the only way that Communism can survive is by adopting the principles of democracy. That is the same thing as saying that the only way in which a wolf can survive is to stop eating meat and become a lamb. And yet Palme lives right next door, Sweden is quite close to the Soviet Union. I think that he, and Mitterrand, and the Italian socialists will live to the day when they will be in the position that Portugal's Mario Soares is in today. Soares's situation, by the way, is not yet at its worst. An even more terrible future awaits him and his party. Only the Russian socialists—the Mensheviks and the Socialist Revolutionaries—could have told them of the fate that awaits them. But they cannot tell of it: they are all dead; they've all been killed. Read *The Gulag Archipelago.*

Of course in the present situation the Communists have to use various disguises. Sometimes we hear words like the "popular front," at other times "dialogue with Christianity." For Communists a dialogue with Christianity! In the Soviet Union this dialogue was a simple matter: they used machine guns and revolvers. And today, in Portugal, unarmed Catholics are stoned by the Communists. This is dialogue . . . And when the French and the Italian Communists say that they are going to have a dialogue, let them only get into power and we shall see what this dialogue will look like.

When I traveled to Italy this past April, I was amazed to see hammers and sickles painted on the doors of churches, insults to priests scrawled on the doors of their houses. In general, offensive Communist graffiti cover the walls of Italian cities. This is today, before they have attained power. This is today . . . When Italy's leaders were in Moscow, Palmiro Togliatti agreed to all of Stalin's executions. Just let them have power in Italy and we shall see what the dialogue will look like then.

All of the Communist Parties, upon attaining power, have become completely merciless. But at the stage before they achieve power, it is necessary to use disguises.

We Russians, with our historical experience, find

it tragic to see what is going on in Portugal. We were always told, "Well, this happened to you Russians. It's just that you couldn't maintain democracy in your country. You had it for eight months and then it was stifled. That's Eastern Europe for you." But look at Portugal, at the very westernmost edge of Europe, and what do we see there? A kind of caricature, a slightly altered version of what happened in Russia. For us it sounds like a re-run. We recognize what's going on and can make the proper substitutions, placing our socialists in Soares's position.

The same things were said in Russia. The Bolsheviks pursued power under the slogan "All Power to the Constituent Assembly." But when the elections took place, they got 25 percent of the vote, and so they dispersed the Constituent Assembly. The Communists in Portugal got 12 percent of the vote. So they made their parliament entirely powerless. What irony: the socialists have won the elections. Soares is the leader of the victorious party. Yet he has been deprived of his own newspaper. Just imagine: the leader of a victorious party has been stripped of his own newspaper! And the fact that an assembly has been elected and will sit in session has no significance whatever. Yet the Western press writes seriously that the first free elections took place in Portugal. Lord save us from such free elections!

Specific instances of duplicity, of trickery, can change of course from one set of circumstances to another. But we recognize the Communist character in the episode when the Portuguese military leaders, who are allegedly not Communists, decided to settle the dispute within the newspaper *República* in the following manner. "Come at twelve o'clock tomorrow," they said, "we'll open the doors for you and you settle it all as you see fit." But they opened the doors at ten o'clock and for some reason only the Communists, not the socialists, knew of this. The Communists entered, burned all the incriminating documents, and then the socialists arrived. Ah yes, it was of course only an error. An accident, they didn't check the time . . .

These are the sort of tricks—and there are thousands—which make up the history of the Russian Revolution. There will be many more such incidents in Portugal. Take the following example: the current military leadership of Portugal, in order not to lose Western assistance (they have already ruined Portugal and there is nothing to eat, so they need help), have declared, "Yes, we will keep our multi-party system." And the unfortunate Soares, the leader of the victorious party, now has to demonstrate that he is pleased with this declaration in favor of a multi-party system. But on the same day the same source declared that the construction of a classless society will begin immediately. Anyone who is the least bit familiar with Marxism knows that "classless society" implies that there will not be any parties. That is to say, on the very same day they said: There will be a multi-party system and we will suppress every party. But the former is heard and the latter is not. Everybody repeats only that there will be a multi-party system. This is a typical Communist method.

Portugal has, in effect, fallen out of NATO already. I don't wish to be a prophet of doom but these events are irreversible. Very shortly Portugal will be considered a member of the Warsaw Pact. It is painful to look at this tragic and ironic repetition of Communist methods at opposite ends of Europe, sixty years apart. In just a few months we see the stifling of a democracy which had only begun to get on its feet.

The question of war is also well elucidated in Communist and Marxist literature. Let me show you how Communism regards the question of war. I quote Lenin: "We cannot support the slogan 'Peace' since it is a totally muddled one and a hindrance to the revolutionary struggle." (Letter to Alexandra Kollontai, July 1915.) "To reject war in principle is un-Marxist. Who objectively stands to gain from the slogan 'Peace'? In any case, not the revolutionary proletariat." (Letter to Alexander Shliapnikov, November 1914.) "There is no point in proposing a benign program of pious wishes for peace without at the same time placing at the forefront the call for illegal organization and the summons to civil war." This is Communism's view of war. War is necessary. War is an instrument for achieving a goal.

But unfortunately for Communism, this policy ran up against the American atomic bomb in 1945. Then the Communists changed their tactics and suddenly became advocates of peace at any cost. They started to convoke peace congresses, to circulate petitions for peace; and the Western world fell for this deceit. But the goal, the ideology, remained the same: to destroy your system, to destroy the way of life known in the West.

But they could not risk this in the face of your nuclear superiority. So they substituted one concept for another: what is not war, they said, is peace. That is, they opposed war to peace. But this is a mistake, only a part of the antithesis is opposed to the thesis. When an open war is impossible, oppression can continue quietly behind the scenes. Terrorism. Guerrilla warfare, violence, prisons, concentration camps. I ask you: Is this peace?

The true antipode of peace is violence. And those who want peace in the world should remove not only war from the world but also violence. If there is no open war but there is still violence, that is not peace.

As long as in the Soviet Union, in China, and in other Communist countries there is no limit to the use of violence—and now we find India joining in (it appears that Indira Gandhi has learned much from her trip to Moscow; she has mastered these methods very well and is now adding another 400 million people to this continent of tyranny)—as long as there is no limit to this use of violence, as long as nothing restrains it over this tremendous land mass (more than half of humanity), how can you consider yourselves secure?

America and Europe together are not yet an island in the ocean—I won't go so far as to say that. But America together with Europe is now a minority, and the process is still continuing. Until the public in those Communist countries can keep a check on the government and can have an opinion on what the government does—now it doesn't have the slightest idea what the government is up to—until that time comes, the West, and the world in general, has no guarantee at all.

We have another proverb in Russia: "Catch on you will when you're tumbling downhill."

I understand that you love freedom, but in our crowded world you have to pay a tax for freedom. You cannot love freedom for yourselves alone and quietly agree to a situation where the majority of humanity, spread over the greater part of the globe, is subjected to violence and oppression.

The Communist ideology is to destroy your social order. This has been their aim for 125 years and it has never changed; only the methods have changed a little. When there is détente, peaceful co-existence, and trade, they will still insist: the ideological war must continue! And what is ideological war? It is a concentration of hatred, a continued repetition of the oath to destroy the Western world. Just as in the Roman senate a famous speaker ended every speech with the statement: "Furthermore, Carthage must be destroyed," so today, with every act— détente, trade, or whatever—the Communist press, as well as thousands of speakers at closed lectures, all repeat: "Furthermore, capitalism must be destroyed."

It is easy to understand, it's only human that people living in prosperity doubt the necessity of taking steps—here and now in our state of prosperity—to defend themselves. For even in prosperity one must be on guard.

If I were to enumerate all the treaties that have been violated by the Soviet Union, it would take me another whole speech. I understand that when your statesmen sign some treaty with the Soviet Union or China you want to believe that it will be carried out. But the Poles who signed a treaty with the Communists in Riga in 1921 also wanted to believe that the treaty would be carried out, and they were stabbed in the back. Estonia, Latvia, and Lithuania, which signed treaties of friendship with the Soviet Union, also wanted to believe that they would be carried out, but these countries were all swallowed.

And the people who sign these treaties with you now—these very men and no others—simultaneously give orders for persons to be confined in mental hospitals and prisons. Why should they be different toward you? Surely not out of love for

you? Why should they act honorably and nobly toward you when they crush their own people? The
advocates of détente have yet to explain this.

You want to believe and so you cut down on your
armies and your research. There used to be an Institute for the Study of the Soviet Union—at least
there was one such institute. You know so little
about the Soviet Union. It seems dark over there.
These searchlights don't penetrate that far. Knowing nothing, you eliminated the last genuine institute
which could actually study this Soviet society, because there wasn't enough money to support it. But
the Soviet Union is studying you. You are all wide
open here, through the press and Congress. And
they study you all the more, increasing the size of
their staffs in the United States. They follow what's
going on in your institutions. They attend meetings
and conferences; they even visit congressional committees. They study everything.

Of course, peace treaties are very attractive to
those who sign them. They strengthen one's prestige
with the electorate. But the time will come when
the names of these public figures will be erased from
history. Nobody will remember them any longer.
But the Western peoples will have to pay heavily
for these overtrusting agreements.

Is it only a question of showing that détente is needed today, here and now? By no means. There are theoreticians who look very far into the future. The director of the Russian Institute of Columbia University, Marshall Shulman, at a meeting of the Senate Foreign Relations Committee, depicted a radiant future, stating that détente would ultimately lead to cooperation between the United States and the U.S.S.R. in the establishment of a world order. But what sort of new order, in cooperation with insatiable totalitarianism, does this professor want to see established? It won't be your kind in any case.

The principal argument of the advocates of détente is well known: all of this must be done to avoid a nuclear war. But after all that has happened in recent years, I think I can set their minds at ease, and your minds at ease as well: there will not be any nuclear war. What for? Why should there be a nuclear war if for the last thirty years they have been breaking off as much of the West as they wanted—piece after piece, country after country, and the process keeps going on. In 1975 alone four countries were broken off. Four—three in Indochina plus India—and the process keeps going on, very rapidly too. One should be aware of how rapid the tempo is. But let us assume that finally the Western world will understand and say, "No, not one step further." What will happen then?

Let me direct your attention to the following fact: You have theoreticians who say; "The U.S. must stop the process of nuclear armament. We have enough already. Today America has enough nuclear weapons to destroy the other half of the world. Why should we need more than that?" Let the American nuclear specialists reason this way if they want, but for some reason the nuclear specialists of the Soviet Union—and the leaders of the Soviet Union—think differently. Ask your specialists! Leave aside their superiority in tanks and airplanes —where they surpass you by a factor of four, five, or seven. Take the SALT talks alone: in these negotiations your opponent is continually deceiving you. Either he is testing radar in a way which is forbidden by the agreement, or he is violating the limitations on the dimensions of missiles, or he is violating the limitations on their destructive force, or else he is violating the conditions on multiple warheads.

As the proverb says, "Look before you leap, or you will have bruises to keep."

At one time there was no comparison between the strength of the U.S.S.R. and your own. Then it became equal to yours. Now, as all recognize, it is becoming superior to yours. Perhaps today the ratio is just greater than equal, but soon it will be 2 to 1. Then 3 to 1. Finally it will be 5 to 1. I'm not a specialist in this area, and I suppose you're not specialists either, but this can hardly be accidental. I think that if the armaments they had before were enough, they would not have driven things further. There must be some reason for it. With such nuclear superiority it will be possible to block the use of your weapons, and on some unlucky morning they will declare: "Attention. We're sending our troops into Europe, and if you make a move, we will annihilate you." And this ratio of 3 to 1 or 5 to 1 will have its effect: you will not make a move. Indeed, theoreticians will be found to say, "If only we could have that blessed silence . . ."

To make a comparison with chess, this is like two players who are sitting at a chessboard, one of whom has a tremendously high opinion of himself and a rather low opinion of his opponent. Of course, he thinks he will outplay his opponent. He thinks he is so clever, so calculating, so inventive, that he will certainly win. He sits there, calculating his moves. With these two knights he will make four forks. He can hardly wait for his opponent to move.

He's squirming on his chair from happiness. He takes off his glasses, wipes them, and puts them back on again. He doesn't even admit the possibility that his opponent may be more clever. He doesn't even see that his pawns are being taken one after the other and that his castle is under threat. It all seems to him, "Aha, that's what we'll do. We'll set Moscow, Peking, Pyongyang, Hanoi one against the other."

But what a joke! No one will do any such thing! In the meantime, you've been outplayed in West Berlin, you've been very skillfully outplayed in Portugal. In the Near East you're being outplayed. One shouldn't have such a low opinion of one's opponent.

But even if this chess player is able to win the game on the board, he forgets to raise his eyes, carried away as he is by the game; he forgets to look at his opponent and doesn't see that he has the eyes of a killer. And if this opponent cannot win the game on the board, he will take a club from behind his back and shatter the skull of our chess player, ending the game that way. Our very calculating chess player also forgets to raise his eyes to the barometer. It has fallen. He doesn't see that it's already dark outside, that clouds are gathering, that a hurricane is rising. That's what it means to be too self-confident in chess.

In addition to the grave political situation in the world today, we are also witnessing the emergence of a crisis of unknown nature, one completely new, and entirely non-political. We are approaching a major turning point in world history, in the history of civilization. It has already been noted by specialists in various areas. I could compare it only with the turning from the Middle Ages to the modern era, a shift in our civilization. It is a juncture at which settled concepts suddenly become hazy, lose their precise contours, at which our familiar and commonly used words lose their meaning, become empty shells, and methods which have been reliable for many centuries no longer work. It's the sort of turning point where the hierarchy of values which we have venerated, and which we use to determine what is important to us and what causes our hearts to beat is starting to rock and may collapse.

These two crises, the political crisis of today's world and the oncoming spiritual crisis, are occurring at the same time. It is our generation that will have to confront them. The leadership of your country, which is entering the third century of existence as a nation, will perhaps have to bear a burden greater than ever before in American history. Your leaders will need profound intuition, spiritual foresight, high qualities of mind and soul. May God grant that in those times you will have at the helm personalities as great as those who created your country.

In recent weeks, I have traveled through various states, and I am aware that the two cities in which I have made my addresses—Washington and New York—do not reflect your country as a whole with its tremendous diversity and possibilities. Just as old St. Petersburg did not express the whole of Russia, just as Moscow does not reflect the Soviet Union of today, and just as Paris more than once abused its claim to represent all of France.

I was profoundly impressed by my contact with those places which are, and have always been, the wellsprings of your history. It makes one think that the men who created your country never lost sight of their moral bearings. They did not laugh at the absolute nature of the concepts of "good" and "evil." Their practical policies were checked against that moral compass. And how surprising it is that a practical policy computed on the basis of moral considerations turned out to be the most farsighted and the most salutary. This is true even though in the short term one may wonder: Why all this morality? Let's just get on with the immediate job.

The leaders who created your country never said: "Let slavery reign right next door, and we will enter into détente with it as long as it doesn't come here."

I have traveled enough through the different states of your country and in its various regions to have became convinced that the American heartland is healthy, strong, and broad in its outlook. I am convinced that these healthy, generous, and inexhaustible forces will help you to elevate the whole style of your government leadership.

Yet, when one travels in your country and sees your free and independent life, all the dangers which I talked about today seem imaginary. I've talked to people, and I see this is so. In your wide-open spaces even I get a little infected, the dangers seem somehow unreal. On this continent it is hard to believe all the things which are happening in the world. But, ladies and gentlemen, this carefree life cannot continue in your country any more than in ours. The destinies of our two countries are going to be extremely difficult, and it is better to prepare for this beforehand.

I understand, I sense that you're tired. But you have not yet really suffered the terrible trials of the twentieth century which have rained down on the old continent. You're tired, but not as tired as we are, crushed for sixty years. You're tired, but the Communists who want to destroy your system are not; they're not tired at all.

I understand that this is the most unfavorable time to come to this country and to make this sort of address. But if it were a better, more appropriate time, there would be no need for me to speak.

Precisely because this is the worst possible time I have come to tell you about our experience over there. If our experience in the East could flow over to you by itself, it would be unnecessary for me to assume the unpleasant and inappropriate role of orator. I am a writer, and I would prefer to sit and write books.

But a concentration of world evil is taking place, full of hatred for humanity. It is fully determined to destroy your society. Must you wait until it comes to smash through your borders, until the young men of America have to fall defending the borders of their continent?

After my first address, as always, there were some superficial comments in the newspapers which did not really get to its essence. One of them asserted that I had come here with an appeal to the United States to liberate *us* from Communism. Anyone who has followed what I have said and written these many years, first in the Soviet Union and now in the West, will know that I've always said the exact opposite. I have appealed to my own countrymen— those whose courage has failed at difficult moments, and who have looked imploringly to the West—and urged them: "Don't wait for assistance, and don't ask for it; we must stand on our own feet. The West has enough troubles without us. If they support us, they have our heartfelt thanks. But to plead for help, to appeal for it—never."

I said the last time that two processes are occurring in the world today. One is a process of spiritual liberation in the U.S.S.R. and in the other Communist countries. The second is the assistance being extended by the West to the Communist rulers, a process of concessions, of détente, of yielding whole countries. And I only said: "Remember, we have to pull ourselves up by our own efforts—but if you do defend us, you defend your own future."

We are slaves there from birth. We are born slaves. I'm not young any more, and I myself was born a slave; this is even more true for those who are younger. We are slaves, but we are striving for freedom. You, however, were born free. So why do you let yourselves be used by slavery? Why do you help our slaveowners?

In my last address I only requested one thing and I make the same request now: when they bury us in the ground alive—I compared the forthcoming European agreement with a mass grave for all the countries of Eastern Europe—as you know, this is a very unpleasant sensation: your mouth gets filled with earth while you're still alive—please do not send them shovels. Please do not send them the latest earth-moving equipment.

By a peculiar coincidence, the very day when I was giving my address in Washington, Mikhail Suslov was talking with your senators in the Kremlin. And he said, "In fact, the significance of our trade is more political than economic. We can get along without your trade." That's a lie. The whole existence of our slaveowners from beginning to end relies on Western economic assistance. As I said the last time, beginning with the first spare parts used to reconstruct our factories in the 1920's, from the construction in Magnitostroy, Dneprostroy, the automobile and tractor factories built during the first five-year plans, on into the postwar years and to this day, what they need from you is economically absolutely indispensable—not politically, but economically indispensable—to the Soviet system. The Soviet economy has an extremely low level of efficiency. What is done here by a few people, by a few machines, in our country takes tremendous crowds of workers and enormous amounts of material. Therefore, the Soviet economy cannot deal with every problem at once: war, space (which is part of the war effort), heavy industry, light industry, and at the same time the need to feed and clothe its own population. The forces of the entire Soviet economy are concentrated on war, where you don't help them. But everything lacking, everything needed to fill the gaps, everything necessary to feed the people, or for other types of industry, they get from you. So indirectly you are helping their military preparations. You are helping the Soviet police state.

I'll give you an example of the clumsiness of the Soviet economy: What kind of country is it, what kind of great power, with tremendous military potential, that conquers outer space but has nothing to sell? All heavy equipment, all complex and delicate technology, is purchased abroad. Then it must be an agricultural country? Not at all; it also has to buy grain. What then can we sell? What kind of economy is it? Can we sell anything which has been created by socialism? No! Only that which God put in the Russian ground at the very beginning, that's what we squander and that's what we sell. When all this comes to an end, there won't be anything left to sell.

The president of the AFL-CIO, George Meany, has quite rightly said that it is not loans which the United States gives to the Soviet Union, it is economic assistance, foreign aid, given at a lower interest level than what American workers can get for their home mortgages. That is direct aid.

But this is not all. I said in my last address, and would like to repeat, that we have to look at every event from the other point of view—from the point of view of the Soviet Union. Our country takes your assistance, but in the schools they teach and in the newspapers they write and in lectures they say: "Look at the Western world, it's beginning to rot. Look at the economy of the Western world, it's coming to an end. The great predictions of Marx, Engels, and Lenin are coming true. Capitalism is breathing its last. It's already dead. And our socialist economy is flourishing. It has demonstrated once and for all the triumph of Communism." I think, ladies and gentlemen, and I particularly address

[86]

those of you who have a socialist outlook, that we should at least permit this socialist economy to prove its superiority. Let's allow it to show that it is advanced, that it is omnipotent, that it has defeated you, that it has overtaken you. Let us not interfere with it. Let us stop selling to it and giving it loans. If it's all that powerful, then let it stand on its own feet for ten or fifteen years. Then we will see what it looks like. I can tell you what it will look like. I am being quite serious now. When the Soviet economy will no longer be able to deal with everything, it will have to reduce its military preparations. It will have to abandon the useless space effort and it will have to feed and clothe its own people. And the system will be forced to relax.

Thus, all I ask you is that as long as this Soviet economy is so proud, so flourishing, and yours is so rotten and so moribund—stop helping it. When has a cripple ever helped along an athlete?

Another distortion appeared in your press with respect to my last address. Someone wrote that "one more advocate of the Cold War has come here. One more person has arrived to call on us to resume the Cold War." That is a misunderstanding. The Cold War—the war of hatred—is still going on, but only on the Communist side. What is the Cold War? It's a war of abuse and they still abuse you. They trade with you, they sign agreements and treaties, but they still abuse you, they still curse you. In sources which you can read, and even more in those which are unavailable to you, and which you don't hear of, in the depths of the Soviet Union, the Cold War has never stopped, not for one second. They never call you anything but "American imperialists." One day, if they want, all the Soviet newspapers could say that America wants to subjugate the world and our people would have nowhere to get any other information. Do I call upon you to return to the Cold War? By no means, God forbid! What for? The only thing I'm asking you to do is to give the Soviet economy a chance to develop. Do not bury us in the ground, just let the Soviet economy develop, and then let's see.

But can the free and varied Western system follow such a policy? Can all the Western countries together say: It's true, let us stop competing. Let us stop playing up to them. Let us stop elbowing each other and clamoring, "Me, me, let me have a concession, please give it to me" . . . . It's very possible that this cannot be done. And if this sort of unity cannot be achieved in the West, if, in the frenzied competition of one company with another, they will continue to rush in loans and advanced technology, if they will present earth-moving equipment to our gravediggers, then I'm afraid that Lenin will turn out to have been right. He said: "The bourgeoisie will sell us rope, and then we will let the bourgeoisie hang itself."

In ancient times trade used to begin with the meeting of two persons who had come out of a forest or had arrived by sea. They would show one another that they didn't have a stone or club in their hand, that they were unarmed; as a sign of this, each extended an open hand. This was the beginning of the handclasp. Today's word "détente" literally means a reduction in the tension of a taut rope. (What an ominous coincidence: a rope again!)

So "détente" means a relaxation of tension. But I would say that what we need instead is an image of the open hand. Relations between the Soviet Union and the United States should be such that there would be no deceit in the question of armaments, that there would be no concentration camps, no psychiatric wards for healthy people. Relations should be such that the throats of our women would no longer be constricted with tears, that there would be an end to the incessant ideological warfare waged against you, and that an address such as mine today would in no way be an exception.

People would simply be able to come to you from the Soviet Union, from China, and from other Communist countries and would be able to talk freely, without any tutoring from the KGB, without any special approval from the Central Committee of the party. Rather, they would simply come of their own accord and would tell you the truth about what is going on in these countries.

This would be, I say, a period in which we would be able to present "open hands" to each other.

GENTLEMEN:

HERE, in the Senate Office Building I must begin by saying that I have not forgotten the high, indeed the exceptional, honor paid me by the United States Senate in twice endeavoring to declare me an honorary citizen of the United States.

I take this to mean that you had in mind not only myself as an individual but also the millions of my fellow countrymen who have been deprived of rights, and even those in the other Communist countries, those millions who have never been able, and are still unable, to express their opinions in the press, in parliaments, or at international conferences.

As I convey to you my gratitude for the decisions

This speech was delivered by Mr. Solzhenitsyn to members of the Senate and the House of Representatives in Washington, D.C.

of the United States Senate concerning myself, I am all the more conscious of my responsibility as a spokesman for those others, a responsibility almost too massive for the shoulders of a single human being. But I have never lost sight of the suffering, the striving and the hopes of those voiceless millions, and have had no aim in life other than to give them expression, and this lends me strength for my public appearances in this country and for my appearance before you today. For the time being, there are few people in the Communist countries who speak out publicly, but millions understand the loathsome nature of the system and feel a revulsion toward it. Whoever can "votes with his feet," simply fleeing from this mass violence and destruction.

I see before me today not only members of the Senate but also a group of Representatives. Thus, I am speaking for the first time to participants in your country's legislative process whose influence in recent years has spread far beyond the limits of American history.

In virtually every respect, our Russian historical experience has been almost the opposite of yours. The innumerable events that have befallen us in the twentieth century have enriched our Russian experience in an unfortunate way, and now they seem to confront you from the future. It is that much more crucial that we persistently and sincerely try to convey our respective experience to one another. One of today's most terrible dangers is precisely that the destinies of the world are entangled as never before, so that events or mistakes in one part of the world are immediately felt in all the others. At the same time, the exchange of information and of opinions between populations is blocked by iron barriers on the one side, while on the other it is distorted by distance, paucity of information, narrowness of outlook, or deliberate misrepresentation by observers and commentators.

In my few addresses in your country I have attempted to break through that wall of disastrous unawareness or nonchalant superiority. I have tried to convey to your countrymen the constrained breathing of the inhabitants of Eastern Europe in these weeks when an amicable agreement of diplomatic shovels will inter in a common grave bodies that are still breathing. I have tried to explain to Americans that 1973, the tender dawn of détente, was precisely the year when the starvation rations in Soviet prisons and concentration camps were reduced even further. And in recent months, when more and more Western speechmakers have pointed to the beneficial consequences of détente, the Soviet Union has adopted a novel and important improvement in its system of punishment: to retain their glorious supremacy in the invention of forced-labor camps, Soviet prison specialists have now established a new form of solitary confinement—forced labor in solitary cells. That means cold, hunger, lack of fresh air, insufficient light, and impossible work norms; the failure to fulfill these norms is punished by confinement under even more brutal conditions.

Alas, such is human nature that we never feel the sufferings of others, and they never darken our temporary well-being, until they become our own. I am not certain that in my addresses here I have succeeded in conveying the breath of that terrible reality to a complacently prosperous American society. But I have done what I could and what I consider my duty. So much the worse if the justice of my warnings becomes evident only some years hence.

Your country has just recently passed through the extended ordeal of Vietnam, which exhausted and divided your society. I can say with certainty that this ordeal was the least of a long chain of similar trials which awaits you in the near future.

Whether or not the United States so desires, it

has risen to the peak of world history and carries the burden of leadership for at least half the world. The United States has not had a thousand-year preparation for this task. Perhaps the two hundred years of your existence has not been time enough to produce a sense of national awareness. Meanwhile, the load of obligations and responsibilities has fallen on you unbidden.

That is why, members of the Senate and of the House of Representatives, each one of you is not just an ordinary member of an ordinary parliament—you have been elevated to a particularly high position in the contemporary world. I would like to convey to you how we, the subjects of Communist states, look upon your words, deeds, proposals, and enactments, which are made known to the world through the media. We sometimes greet them with passionate approval, at other times with horror and despair. But we never have a chance to respond aloud.

Perhaps some of you, in your minds, still consider yourselves to represent only your state or party. But, from over there, from afar, we do not perceive these differences. We do not look upon you as Democrats or Republicans, or as representatives of the Eastern Seaboard or the West Coast or the Midwest; we see you as statesmen, each of whom will play a direct and decisive role in the further course of world history, as it proceeds toward tragedy or salvation.

In the oncoming conjunction of a world political crisis with the present changes in a humanity exhausted and choked by a false hierarchy of values, you or your successors on Capitol Hill will have to confront—you are already facing—problems of overwhelming difficulty, incomparably greater than the short-term calculations of diplomacy, of inter-party struggles, or of the clash between President and Congress. There is but one choice: to rise to the tasks of the age.

Very soon, only too soon, your country will stand in need of not just exceptional men but of *great* men. Find them in your souls. Find them in your hearts. Find them in the depths of your country.

Speeches to the British

MICHAEL CHARLTON: *Alexander Isaevich, when Mr. Brezhnev and the Politburo decided to exile you abroad rather than send you once more to a concentration camp, they must have believed that you would do less damage to the Communist state outside the Soviet Union than inside it. So I wonder if you believe that time will prove that judgment to be correct?*

ALEXANDER SOLZHENITSYN:

IN the way you put that question there is a certain false assumption. If one puts the question in this way we assume that the Politburo is all-powerful

---

This is the text of an interview with Mr. Solzhenitsyn conducted by Michael Charlton for the BBC program *Panorama*. The interview was subsequently aired in the United States on William F. Buckley's *Firing Line*.

and independent in the decisions it makes, that it is free to decide one way or another. I must say that at the time of my exile the situation was very unusual. I wrote about this some time ago. In the autumn of 1973 the support of Western public opinion for Sakharov and myself in our head-on confrontation, as I have called it, was so powerful, so unyielding, firm, steadfast, support such as the West had not demonstrated for a long time, that the Soviet Politburo simply took fright. It did not have complete freedom of choice either to keep me in prison *or* to exile me; they simply took fright at this anger, this storm of indignation in the West, and were forced to give way. This was a forced concession. For that reason, I think that now, even if they regret it—and I imagine they do regret it—we must remember that they, in effect, had no choice. That was a rare moment when the West demonstrated unprecedented firmness and forced them to retreat.

On the other hand, they would be right, wouldn't they, if you felt that your warnings, or your beliefs, fell upon deaf ears in the West. You would then cease to be relevant, and that presumably is what they hope for?

Yes, if one looks at it from this point of view, you are right. My warnings, the warnings of others, Sakharov's very grave warning directly from the Soviet Union, these warnings go unheeded; most of them fall, as it were, on the ears of the deaf, people who do not want to hear them. Once I used to hope that experience of life could be handed on from nation to nation, and from one person to another, but now I am beginning to have doubts about this. Perhaps everyone is fated to live through every experience himself in order to understand.

Well, you are now in the unique position to watch a debate in both East and West which to a large extent has been inspired, or has been focused, by your own experiences and writings. How important is the experience of the Russian people for the West?

In actual fact our Russian experience—when I use the word "Russian" I always differentiate it from the word "Soviet"—I have in mind even pre-Soviet, pre-revolutionary experience—in actual fact it is vitally important for the West, because by some chance of history we have trodden the same path seventy or eighty years before the West. And now it is with a rather strange sensation that we look at what is happening to you; many social phenomena that happened in Russia before its collapse are being repeated. Our experience of life is of vital importance to the West, but I am not convinced that you are capable of assimilating it without having gone through it to the end yourselves.

Give me an example of what you mean by the Russian experience being repeated in the West.

You know, one could quote here many examples; for one, a certain retreat by the older generation, yielding their intellectual leadership to the younger generation. It is against the natural order of things for those who are youngest, with the least experience of life, to have the greatest influence in directing the life of society. One can say then that this is what forms the spirit of the age, the current of public opinion, when people in authority, well-known professors and scientists, are reluctant to enter into an argument even when they hold a different opinion. It is considered embarrassing to put forward one's counterarguments, lest one become involved. And so there is a certain abdication of responsibility, which is typical here where there is complete freedom. Let us take the press, writers, journalists, who enjoy great freedom (incidentally Russia also enjoyed great freedom; the West has a completely false view of Russia before the Revolution) and meanwhile lose their sense of responsibility before history, before their own people. There is now a universal adulation of revolutionaries, the more so the more extreme they are! Similarly, before the revolution, we had in Russia, if not a cult of terror, then a fierce defense of terrorists. People in good positions—intellectuals, professors, liberals—spent a great deal of effort, anger, and indignation in defending terrorists. And then the paralysis of government power. I could give you many more analogies.

But, as you say, it is the West which has made it possible for people like you to survive. In view of what you have just said, how would you say that your two years in the West have reshaped your views? You are obviously more pessimistic now than you were when you came.

I must say that in relation to the West my generation—I am not going to speak only about myself personally, and when I say my generation, I have in mind people who shared my fate, that is to say, the soldiers of the Second World War and then the prisoners, this was after all the common fate of so many. As I was saying, my generation went through several stages. In the fifties, after the end of the war, we literally worshipped the West. We looked upon the West as being the sun of freedom, a fortress of the spirit, our hope, our ally. We all thought that it would be difficult to liberate ourselves, but that the West would help us to rise from slavery. Gradually, in the course of decades and years, this faith began to waver and to fade. We received information about the West only with difficulty, but we learned to listen even through the fiercest jamming, for example, to your BBC. We realized with bewilderment that the West was not showing that firmness and that interest in freedom in *our* country as well; it was as if the West was separating its freedom from our fate. Before I was exiled, I already had strong doubts as to whether it was realistic to look to the West for help. It is precisely on this that my opinions differ from those of Sakharov; Sakharov considers that help from the West is of decisive importance for our liberation, while I believe that we can obtain freedom only by relying upon ourselves, and that one can place practically no hopes on the West. Unfortunately, when I came here, my doubts increased very rapidly. But the point is, of course, that during these two years the West itself has gone through a good deal. During these two years the West has become much weaker in relation to the East. The West has made so many concessions that now a repetition of the angry campaign which got me out of prison is practically impossible. I would say that the campaign to get Sakharov to Stockholm was almost as strong, yet it didn't help, because the West itself has become weak over this period. Its position has become weaker. Moscow now takes infinitely less note of the West.

Can I suggest that perhaps one of the difficulties in your own case is that you've become a controversial figure in the West. You are no longer the quiet tourist in the West. You are in some respects an impassioned critic. And I think that the people in the West who criticize you—and, of course, not all do—believe that you are asking for a return to something in Russia that is plainly impossible, a return to a patriarchal kind of Russia, a return to Orthodoxy. Are those criticisms that you accept?

You know, that is one of the consequences of the weak sense of responsibility of the press. The press does not feel responsibility for its judgments, it makes judgments and attaches labels with the greatest of ease. Mediocre journalists simply make headlines of their conclusions, which suddenly become generally accepted. You have just enumerated several propositions and practically all of them are not true. First, I am not a critic of the West. I repeat that for nearly all our lives we worshipped the West —note the word "worshipped." We did not admire it, we worshipped it. I am not a critic of the West. I am a critic of the weakness of the West. I am a critic of a fact which we can't comprehend: how one can lose one's spiritual strength, one's will power and, possessing freedom, not value it, not be willing to make sacrifices for it. A second label— just as common—was pinned on me: that I wanted to return to a patriarchal way of life. Well, as I see it, apart from the half-witted, no normal person could ever propose a return to the past, because it's clear to any normal person that one can only move forward. That means that choice lies only between those movements which go forward and not backward. It is quite easy to imagine that some journalist writing mostly about women's fashions thought up this headline, and so the story gets around that I am calling for a patriarchal way of life. I'll just cite one more example: take the word "nationalist"—it has become almost meaningless. It is used constantly. Everyone flings it around, but what is a "nationalist"? If someone suggests that his country should have a large army, conquer the countries which surround it, should go on expanding its empire, that sort of person is a nationalist. But if, on the contrary, I suggest that my country should free all the peoples it has conquered, should disband the army, should stop all aggressive actions—who am I? A nationalist! If you love England, what are you? A nationalist! And when are you not a nationalist? When you *hate* England, then you are not a nationalist.

Well, you make the point very eloquently that you're not going back in the sense of a return to the old Russian imperialism, but I'm not sure how you go forward as you claim you would. What is the way out of this world of tensions and oppression in the Soviet Union that you so eloquently describe? If the West cannot help, what is the way forward for the Russian people? What will happen?

You have just used the expression "for the Russian people," by which you mean the Soviet Union—do I understand you correctly? You know, two and three years ago this question was topical. That is to say, it was possible to believe that we inhabitants of the Soviet Union could sit down and consider our future. The Soviet leadership was experiencing so many difficulties, so many failures, that it had to seek some way out, and indeed I thought that the way out was to seek the path of evolution, certainly not the path of *revolution*, not an explosion. On this, Sakharov and I agree: an evolutionary, smooth path which would offer a way out of this terrible system. However, today, all these suggested solutions have lost their practical value. Over the last two years, terrible things have happened. The West has given up not only four, five, or six countries; the West has given up all its world positions. The West has given everything away so impetuously, has done so much to strengthen the tyranny in our country, that today all these questions are no longer relevant in the Soviet Union. Opposition has remained, but I have already said many times that our movement of opposition and spiritual revival, like any spiritual process, is slow. But your capitulations, like all political processes, move very quickly. The speed of your capitulations has so rapidly overtaken the pace of our moral regeneration that at the moment the

Soviet Union can only move along one path: the flourishing of totalitarianism. It would be more appropriate if it were not you asking me which way Russia—or rather, the Soviet Union (let us not get the two mixed)—will go, but if I were to ask you which way the West is going. Because at the moment the question is not how the Soviet Union will find a way out of totalitarianism but how the West will be able to avoid the same fate. How will the West be able to withstand the unprecedented force of totalitarianism? That is the problem.

Why do you think that people in the West have begun to feel uneasy with you? This brings me, in view of what you've just said, to the question of spiritual regeneration, moral regeneration: what is the central point for which you stand? After this enormously varied experience that you've had—you've been a teacher, a decorated war hero, an officer in the Soviet Army, a cancer patient, a political prisoner in concentration camps—what is the central point, in all that you say, that you stand for?

Perhaps, if one speaks of my life experience, then I would say that my outlook on life has been formed largely in concentration camps—that part of my life which is reflected in *The Gulag Archipelago*. I don't know whether Western listeners would find my words embarrassing—it is difficult for me to judge this kind of reaction—but I would put it this way: those people who have lived in the most terrible conditions, on the frontier between life and death, be it people from the West or from the East, all understand that between good and evil there is an irreconcilable contradiction, that it is not one and the same thing—good or evil—that one cannot build one's life without regard to this distinction. I am surprised that pragmatic philosophy consistently scorns moral considerations; and nowadays in the Western press we read a candid declaration of the principle that moral considerations have nothing to do with politics. I would remind you that in 1939 England thought differently. If moral considerations were not applicable to politics, then it would be incomprehensible why England went to war with Hitler's Germany. *Pragmatically,* you could have gotten out of the situation, but England chose the moral course, and experienced and demonstrated to the world perhaps the most brilliant and heroic period in its history. But today we have forgotten this; today the English political leaders state quite frankly that they not only recognize *any* power over *any* territory regardless of its moral character but they even *hasten* to recognize it, even try to be the first to do so. Somewhere, in some place, freedom has been lost in Laos, China, or Angola. Tyrants, bandits, puppets have come to power, and pragmatic philosophy says: That doesn't matter, we *have* to recognize them. What is more, one should not consider that the great principles of freedom end at your own frontiers, that as long as *you* have freedom, let the rest have pragmatism. No! Freedom is indivisible and one has to take a moral attitude toward it. Perhaps this is one of the main points of disagreement.

You mention The Gulag Archipelago, *your famous document of life in Stalin's prison camps, which is so full of an overwhelming anger and bitterness. Is the aim of the book simply the destruction of Communist ideology, the destruction of at least its myths; or is it meant to be something more than that?*

A work of art always consists of many parts, many facets and sides, and that means many aims. The artist cannot set himself political aims, the aims of changing a political regime; it may come as a by-product of it, but to fight against untruth and falsehood, to fight against myths, or to fight against an ideology which is hostile to mankind, to fight for our memory, for our memory of what things were like—*that* is the task of the artist. A people which no longer remembers has lost its history and its soul. Yes, the main thing is to re-create. When I sit down to write, my only task is to re-create everything as it happened. And naturally many deductions follow. If today the three volumes of *The Gulag Archipelago* were widely published in the Soviet Union and were freely available to all, then in a very short space of time no Communist ideology would be left. For people who read and understood all this would simply have no more room in their minds for Communist ideology.

In one of your most recent books, you paint a portrait of Lenin in Zurich. Many people, I think, have noted perhaps a similarity between the two of you. The portrait of a powerful character, Lenin, powerless to influence events inside Russia, cut off, isolated, impatient—that does sound rather like you, a powerful figure, living in the same city today, in the West, perhaps powerless to intervene, cut off from your friends in the Soviet Union. Would you be

*surprised, as Lenin was, at a profound change in
the Soviet Union taking place in your lifetime?*

You know, I have been working on the image of
Lenin for forty years. From the moment I conceived
this series of books, I thought of Lenin as one of
the central characters—if not *the* central character.
I gathered every grain of information that I could,
every detail, and my only aim was to re-create him
alive, as he was.

*But in attacking Lenin, of course, you attack the
legitimacy of the whole Soviet government, of the
Bolsheviks themselves. So I just ask you whether you
feel yourself that you, in turn, will become a focus
for this moral, spiritual regeneration inside the Soviet Union. Are you saying that there will be this
kind of spiritual revival, which will in time overthrow the Communist system?*

I don't attack Lenin. I describe him as he was and
for what he is worth. So much incense has been
kindled around him, in your country as well, and
he has been raised to such summits. I show how he
was often shortsighted, how he treated his allies,
collaborators, how weak his ties were with his own

country. I don't attack *him,* but this ideology. The spiritual renaissance of our country lies in our liberation from this deadening, killing ideology.

I'm trying to say: Is it valid to suggest a strong comparison between yourself and Lenin? There he was, waiting in Zurich, unable to do anything about the internal situation and surprised when the change came—he, the great revolutionary. Would you be surprised if the change came?

He was surprised because of his shortsightedness. You can see from my book that because of the narrowness of his party view he had lost sight of the simplest facts, he didn't know that the war was about to start, he was taken unawares by the world war and in the same way by the Revolution. Two years ago I didn't expect any explosion in the Soviet Union; I expected a slow process and it was already taking place. Today, yes, I would be surprised, but I wouldn't be surprised at something else: I wouldn't be surprised at the sudden and imminent fall of the West. I would like to make myself clear: the situation at the moment is such that the Soviet Union's economy is at a war level, that even if it were the unanimous opinion of all the members

of the Politburo not to start a war, this would no
longer be in their power. To avoid this would re-
quire an agonizing change from a monstrous war
economy to a normal peace economy. The situation
now is such that one must think not of what might
happen unexpectedly in the Soviet Union, because
in the Soviet Union nothing will happen unexpectedly. One must think of what might happen unexpectedly in the West. The West is on the verge of a
collapse created by its own hands. This quite naturally makes the question one for you and not for
us.

*I know you say this from the moral standpoint of
a devout Christian, and truth for you is more important than consequences. But you are asking people to say that in the nuclear age; the sword that
hangs over everybody's heads is the electronic one
of nuclear weapons, and I think this is one of the
problems that you face when you are criticized as
being an enemy of détente. What alternatives are
there to dealing with the devil, as you would say, if
the purpose of that is to avoid nuclear catastrophe?*

You know, there was a time at the beginning of
the fifties when this nuclear threat hung over the

world, but the attitude of the West was like granite and the West did not yield. Today this nuclear threat still hangs over both sides, but the West has chosen the wrong path of making concessions. Nuclear war is not even necessary to the Soviet Union. You can be taken simply with bare hands. Why on earth then should one have nuclear war? If you have raised your hands and are giving in, why have nuclear war? They can take you simply like that, without nuclear war. The most important aspect of détente today is that there is no ideological détente. You Westerners simply cannot grasp the power of Soviet propaganda. Today you remain British imperialists who wish to strangle the whole earth. All this is hidden beneath the thin crust of détente; to remove this crust will take only one morning: one single morning. *You* can't be turned away from détente so simply. To turn you away from your present position one would need a year or two. But in the Soviet Union one morning, one command is enough! Newspapers come out with the news that the British imperialists have become so brazen that the situation has become intolerable. And nothing that is being said against you every day will contradict this. And détente—there is no détente, it's just gone. One can't raise the question of détente without ideological détente. If you are hated and hounded in the press, in every single lecture—what sort of détente is that? You are shown up as villains who can be tolerated for perhaps one more day. That is not détente. As for the spirit of Helsinki— may I ask a question in my turn? How do you explain that over the last few months there has been hardly any news coming out of the Soviet Union of the continuing persecution of dissidents. If you will forgive me, I will answer this myself. The journalists have bowed to the spirit of Helsinki. I know for a fact that Western journalists in Moscow, who have been given the right of freer movement, in return for this and because of the spirit of Helsinki, no longer accept information about new persecutions of dissidents in the Soviet Union. What does the spirit of Helsinki and the spirit of détente mean for us within the Soviet Union? The strengthening of totalitarianism. What seems to you to be a milder atmosphere, a milder climate, is for us the strengthening of totalitarianism. Here I would like to give you a few examples, a few fresh examples which you will not have heard about over the radio or read in the papers. May I? Someone went to visit Sakharov; he was killed on his way home on the train. No, it wasn't you, *he* was killed, a Soviet citizen. Someone knocks at the door of Nikolai Kryukov, they have come to fix the gas; he opens the door. They beat him almost to death in his own house because he has defended dissidents and signed protests. All this happens in a flat. But on a street at five o'clock in the afternoon on Lenin Prospect (Lenin!) Malva Landa is seized and dragged into a car. She screamed, "Citizens, I'm being kidnapped," and hundreds of people heard, passed by. They were afraid, because anybody can be seized like that, under the very eyes of passers-by. They shoved her into a car and took her to prison. That's the situation, that's the spirit of Helsinki and détente for us. And so it goes on. In Odessa, Vyacheslav Grunov has been arrested for possessing illicit literature and put into a lunatic asylum. They've released Plyushch, but continue to lock up others. There you have détente and the spirit of Helsinki.

Alexander Isaevich, that was a very powerful feeling in the West, throughout the fifties and sixties, and perhaps now. In fact, a great British philosopher, Bertrand Russell, gave his support to the view "Better Red than dead." But are you saying that this policy of détente was formulated by the Soviet government expressly for the purpose of preventing internal liberalization in the Soviet Union? In other words, the Soviet Union was falling behind economically. In order to catch up it had to import American and West German technology. Otherwise it would have to scrap the whole system. And so it can only catch up by importing its technology from abroad and clamping down internally.

Here, forgive me, there are several questions. Yes, it is the import of technology which is saving the Soviet Union. That's true. But I return to that terrible statement of Bertrand Russell's: "Better Red than dead." Why did he not say it would be better to be brown than dead? There is no difference. All my life and the life of my generation, the life of those who share my views, we all have had one viewpoint: Better to be dead than a scoundrel. In this horrible expression of Bertrand Russell's there is an absence of all moral criteria. Looked at from a short distance, these words allow one to maneuver and to continue to enjoy life. But from a long-term point of view it will undoubtedly destroy those people who think like that. It is a terrible thought. I thank you for quoting this as a striking example.

But you are asking as an alternative for a return

to something like the Cold War tensions. And most people of course welcome détente as a respite from that, a break, something different. Would you agree that the alternative that you propose is likely to be a return to something like the tensions of the Stalin-Khrushchev period?

I would like to emphasize . . . you *think* that this is a respite, but this is an imaginary respite, it's a respite before destruction. As for us, we have no respite at all. We are being strangled even more, with greater determination. You recall the tension of the fifties, but despite that tension you conceded nothing. But today you don't have to be a strategist to understand why Angola is being taken. What for? This is one of the most recent positions from which to wage a world war more successfully—a wonderful position in the Atlantic. The Soviet armed forces have already overtaken the West in many respects and in other respects are on the point of overtaking it. The navy: Britain used to have a navy, now it is the Soviet Union that has the navy, control of the seas, bases; you may call this détente if you like, but after Angola I just can't understand how one's tongue can utter this word! Your Defense Minister has said that after Helsinki the Soviet Union is passing the test. I don't know how many countries have still to be taken, maybe the Soviet tanks have to come to London for your Defense Minister to say at last that the Soviet Union has finally passed the test! Or will it still be taking the exam? I think there is no such thing as détente. Détente is necessary, but détente with open hands. Show that there is no stone in your hands! But your partners with whom you are conducting détente have a stone in their hands and it is so heavy that it could kill you with one single blow. Détente becomes self-deception, that's what it is all about.

Can I ask you finally, as a great Russian patriot, what view you take of your own future?

My own future is closely linked with the fate of my country. I work and have always worked only for it. Our history has been concealed from us, entirely distorted. I am trying to reconstruct this history primarily for my own country. Maybe it will also be useful for the West. My future depends on what will happen to my country. But quite apart from this, the Moscow leaders have particular feelings toward me: so that my own destiny may be decided before that of my country. It is possible of course they may try to get rid of me completely before the fate of my country changes for the better. I sometimes get news of that sort. When I came here I counted on returning very soon, because the Soviet Union *then* was much weaker and the West was much stronger. But over these two years mutual relationships have changed greatly in favor of the Soviet Union.

Mr. Solzhenitsyn, thank you.

[*MARCH* 24, 1976]

THE BBC has been kind enough to invite me to give my opinion, as a foreigner and an exile, on the West as it is today and, in particular, on England. Perhaps an outside view might be able to contribute something fresh. My only hope is that you will not find what I have to say too tedious. I admit I am not all that well acquainted with the internal affairs of your country, but like so many Russians I have always followed Britain's foreign affairs with the keenest interest. I intend to speak frankly and I shall not try to please you or to flatter you in any way. I would ask you to believe me when I say nothing could give me more pleasure than to

This speech was delivered by Mr. Solzhenitsyn over the BBC radio network.

express only admiration. A quarter of a century ago, in the labor camps of Kazakhstan, as we braced ourselves for our hopeless task of stemming the Communist tanks, the West represented the light of freedom. For us the West was not only the strong-hold of the spirit but also the depository of wisdom.

In that very year one of your ministers, Herbert Morrison, somehow managed to persuade *Pravda* to devote an entire page to a statement of his, without any censorship. My God, how eagerly we rushed to where the paper was displayed—a crowd of convicts with shaven heads, filthy jackets, clumsy prison-camp boots.

This was it! At last our subterranean kingdom was going to be pierced with the diamond-bright, diamond-hard ray of truth and hope! At last, Soviet censorship, held for forty years in the grip of a bull-dog's jaws, was to be relaxed. Now he'd make them see the truth! Now he'd stand up for us! But as we read and reread that feeble, insipid article, our hopes subsided slowly. These were the superficial words of someone who had not the slightest idea of the savage structure, the pitiless aims of the Communist world—and of course this was precisely why *Pravda* so generously agreed to print them. We had endured forty years of hell, and this British minister could find no word of hope for us.

The years went by. The decades went by. In spite of the Iron Curtain, views on what was happening in the West, what people were thinking about, kept coming through to us, mainly thanks to the BBC's Russian broadcasts, although they were vigorously jammed. And the more we learned, the more the state of your world perplexed us.

Human nature is full of riddles and contradictions; its very complexity engenders art—and by art I mean the search for something more than simple linear formulations, flat solutions, oversimplified explanations. One of these riddles is: how is it that people who have been crushed by the sheer weight of slavery and cast to the bottom of the pit can nevertheless find the strength to rise up and free themselves, first in spirit and then in body; while those who soar unhampered over the peaks of freedom suddenly lose the taste for freedom, lose the will to defend it, and, hopelessly confused and lost, almost begin to crave slavery. Or again: why is it that societies which have been benumbed for half a century by lies they have been forced to swallow find within themselves a certain lucidity of heart and soul which enables them to see things in their true perspective and to perceive the real meaning of events; whereas societies with access to every kind of information suddenly plunge into lethargy, into a kind of mass blindness, a kind of voluntary self-deception.

This is precisely what we have found to be the correlation between the spiritual development of the East and that of the West. And, alas, the process of your development is five, if not ten times swifter than ours. This is what almost robs mankind of any hope of avoiding a global catastrophe. For years we refused to believe this, thinking that the information which reached us was inadequate. A few years ago I spoke of this with considerable alarm in my Nobel lecture.

And yet, until I came to the West myself and spent two years looking around, I could never have imagined the extreme degree to which the West actually desired to blind itself to the world situation, the extreme degree to which the West had already become a world without a will, a world gradually petrifying in the face of the danger confronting it, a world oppressed above all by the need to defend its freedom.

There is a German proverb which runs *Mut ver-*

loren—alles verloren: "When courage is lost, all is lost." There is another Latin one, according to which loss of reason is the true harbinger of destruction. But what happens to a society in which both these losses—the loss of courage and the loss of reason—intersect? This is the picture which I found the West presents today.

Of course there is a perfectly simple explanation for this process. It is not the superficial one, so fashionable in our day, that man himself is irreproachable and everything is to be blamed on a badly organized society, but a purely human one. Once, it was proclaimed and accepted that above man there was no supreme being, but instead that man was the crowning glory of the universe and the measure of all things, and that man's needs, desires, and indeed his weaknesses were taken to be the supreme imperatives of the universe. Consequently, the only good in the world—the only thing that needed to be done—was that which satisfied our feelings. It was several centuries ago in Europe that this philosophy was born; at the time, its materialistic excesses were explained away by the previous excesses of Catholicism. But in the course of several centuries this philosophy inexorably flooded the entire Western world, and gave it confidence for its colonial conquests, for the seizure of African and Asian slaves. And all this side by side with the outward manifestations of Christianity and the flowering of personal freedom. By the beginning of the twentieth century this philosophy seemed to have reached the height of civilization and reason. And your country, Britain, which had always been the core, the very pearl, of the Western world, gave expression with particular brilliance to this philosophy in both its good and its bad aspects.

In 1914, at the beginning of our ill-fated twentieth century, a storm broke over this civilization, a storm the size and range of which no one at that time could grasp. For four years Europe destroyed herself as never before, and in 1917 a crevasse opened up on the very edge of Europe, a yawning gap enticing the world into an abyss.

The causes for this crevasse are not hard to find: it was the logical result of doctrines that had been bandied about in Europe for ages and had enjoyed considerable success. But this crevasse has something cosmic about it, too, in its unplumbed, unsuspected depths, in its unimaginable capacity for growing wider and wider and swallowing up more and more people.

Forty years earlier Dostoevsky had predicted that

socialism would cost Russia 100 million victims. At the time it seemed an improbable figure. Let me ask the British press to acquaint its readers with the impartial three-page report of the Russian statistician Professor Ivan Kurganov. It was published in the West twelve years ago, but, as is so often the case with matters of social significance, we only notice things that are not contradictory to our own feelings. From Professor Kurganov's analysis, we learn that if Dostoevsky erred, he erred on the side of understatement. From 1917 to 1959 socialism cost the Soviet Union 110 million lives!

When there is a geological upheaval, continents do not topple into the sea immediately. The first thing that happens is that the fatal initial crevasse must appear someplace. For a variety of reasons it so happened that this crevasse first opened up in Russia, but it might just as well have been anywhere else. And Russia, which people considered a backward country, had to leap forward a whole century to overtake all the other countries in the world. We endured inhuman experiences which the Western world—and this includes Britain—has no real conception of and is frightened even to think about.

It is with a strange feeling that those of us who come from the Soviet Union look upon the West of today. It is as though we were neither neighbors on the same planet nor contemporaries. And yet we contemplate the West from what will be *your* future, or we look back seventy years to see our past suddenly repeating itself today. And what we see is always the same as it was then: adults deferring to the opinion of their children; the younger generation carried away by shallow, worthless ideas; professors scared of being unfashionable; journalists refusing to take responsibility for the words they squander so easily; universal sympathy for revolutionary extremists; people with serious objections unable or unwilling to voice them; the majority passively obsessed by a feeling of doom; feeble governments; societies whose defensive reactions have become paralyzed; spiritual confusion leading to political upheaval. What will happen as a result of all this lies ahead of us. But the time is near, and from bitter memory we can easily predict what these events will be.

In the years which followed the worldwide upheaval of 1917, that pragmatic philosophy on which present-day Europe was nourished, with its refusal to take moral decisions, reached its logical conclusion: since there are no higher spiritual forces above us and since I—Man with a capital *M*—am the crowning glory of the universe, then if anyone must perish today, let it be someone else, anybody, but not I, not my precious self, or those who are close to me.

The apocalyptic storm was already raging over the land that used to be Russia when Western Europe speedily extricated itself from that terrible war in its haste to forget and to bring back prosperity, fashions, and the latest dances. Lloyd George actually said: "Forget about Russia. It is our job to ensure the welfare of our own society."

In 1914, when the Western democracies needed help, they were not averse to appealing to Russia. But in 1919 those Russian generals who, for three years, had fought to save the Marne, the Somme, and Verdun, straining Russian resources to the very limit, were refused military aid or even an alliance by their Western friends. Many a Russian soldier lay buried in French soil; others, who had gone to Constantinople, were charged for their rations or had their underwear confiscated in lieu of payment. They were then cajoled into returning to Russia, only to be dealt with by the Bolsheviks, or into embarking for Brazil, only to become semi-slaves on coffee plantations. Unseemly deeds are usually accompanied by high-sounding, even brilliant, justifications. In 1919 no one said openly: "What do your sufferings have to do with us?" Instead, people said: "We have no right to support even the authority of an ally against the wishes of the people."

(Note, however, that in 1945, when millions of Soviet citizens had to be handed over for dispatch to the Gulag Archipelago, this argument was conveniently twisted. "We have no right to carry out the wishes of these millions," it was said, "and to ignore our obligations toward the authorities of an allied country." How easily one's egoism can be satisfied by a handy formula!)

But there were even nobler justifications than these: what was happening in Russia was nothing more than a continuation of all that had happened in eighteenth- and nineteenth-century Europe, a repetition of the general transition from liberalism to socialism. This tendency of ideas to continue on their natural course made people admire them. And so all the aggressive elements, all the influential elements in society—and this was especially the case in Britain—admired what they called the "unprecedented progressive experiment taking place in the U.S.S.R.," while we were being strangled by the cancerous tentacles of the Gulag Archipelago, while millions of hard-working peasants were being sent to die in Siberia in mid-winter. Not very far from where you live, in the Ukraine and in the Kuban, some 6 million peasants, including children, old men and women, died of famine, swollen with hunger and writhing in agony—and this was in peacetime.

Not a single Western newspaper printed photographs or reports of the famine; indeed, your great wit George Bernard Shaw even denied its existence. "Famine in Russia?" he said. "I've never dined so well or so sumptuously as when I crossed the Soviet border." For whole decades your rulers, your members of Parliament, your spokesmen, your journalists, your writers, your leading thinkers managed to ignore the 15-million-strong Gulag Archipelago! Up to thirty books on the Gulag were published in Europe before mine and hardly one of them was even noticed.

There is a borderline beyond which the natural cause of "progressive principles," of "the dawn of a new era," becomes nothing more than calculated, conscious hypocrisy; for this makes life more comfortable to live.

There was, however, one great exception over the last hundred years or so, and that was your struggle with Adolf Hitler, when Britain cast overboard the philosophy of pragmatism or utilitarianism, the philosophy of recognizing any group of gangsters, any puppets, as head of a country so long as they control its territory. Britain assumed a moral stance against Hitler, and it was this that inspired her to one of the most heroic acts of resistance in her history.

A moral stance, even in politics, always safeguards our spirit; sometimes, as we can see, it even protects our very existence. A moral stance can suddenly turn out to be more farsighted than any calculated pragmatism.

Your war with Hitler, however, was not tragic in the Aristotelian sense of the word. Your sacrifices, sufferings, and losses were justified; they did not run counter to the aims of the war. You defended—and successfully defended—precisely that which you intended to defend. But for the people of the U.S.S.R. the war was a tragic war: we were forced to defend our native land with all the strength we could muster and with infinitely greater losses (Kurganov's figures are indisputable: 44 million) and, in so doing, to strengthen all the things that we most loathed —the power of our own executioners, our oppression, our destruction, and, as we can see today, ultimately *your* destruction too. And when those millions of Soviet citizens dared to flee from their oppressors or even to initiate national liberation movements, then our freedom-loving Western allies —and not least among them you British—treacherously disarmed them, bound them, and handed them over to the Communists to be killed. They were sent to labor camps in the Urals, where they mined uranium for the atom bombs which were to be used against you yourselves!

Nor did you shrink from using the butts of your rifles on seventy-year-olds, those very men who had been Britain's allies in the First World War and who were now being hastily handed over to be murdered. From the British Isles alone, one hundred thousand Soviet citizens were forcibly repatriated, while on the continent the number was more than a million. But the most remarkable thing of all was that your free, independent, incorruptible press, your famous *Times, Guardian, New Statesman,* etc., all wittingly shared in the cover-up of this crime, and would have kept silent to this very day had not Professor Julius Epstein from America so tactlessly started his investigations into the fascist techniques that democracies are capable of employing. The conspiracy of the British press was only too successful: indeed, there must be many people in Britain today who have not the faintest idea about this crime committed at the end of the Second World War. But it *was* committed, and it has left a deep and painful mark on the Russian memory.

Twice we helped save the freedom of Western Europe. And twice you repaid us by abandoning us to our slavery. It is clear what you wanted. Once again you wanted to extricate yourselves as quickly as possible from this terrible war; you wanted to rest, you wanted to prosper.

But there was a price to pay. The noble philosophy of pragmatism proclaimed that once again you should close your eyes to a great many things: to the deportation of whole nations to Siberia, to Katyn, to Warsaw (that same country for whose sake the war had started); you should forget Estonia, Latvia, and Lithuania; you should hand over six more of your European sisters into slavery and allow a seventh to be cut in two; at Nuremberg you should sit amicably side by side with judges who were just as much murderers as those on trial and never let this disturb your British sense of justice. Whenever a new tyranny came into existence, however far away—in China, say, or Laos—Britain was always the first to recognize it, eagerly pushing aside all competitors for the honor.

All this required great moral fortitude, and your

society was not found lacking. All one had to do was to repeat again and again the magic formula: "The dawn of a new era." You whispered it. You shouted it. And when you grew sick of it and decided to reaffirm your valor in the eyes of the world and recover your self-respect, then your country manifested incomparable daring—against Iceland, against Spain, countries which could not even answer you back.

Tank columns in East Berlin, Budapest, and Prague declared that they were there "by the will of the people," but not once did the British government recall its ambassadors from any of these places in protest. In Southeast Asia unknown numbers of prisoners have been killed and are still being killed in secret; yet the British ambassadors have not been recalled. Every day in the Soviet Union psychiatrists murder people with their hypodermic syringes merely because they do not think along accepted lines or because they believe in God, and again the British ambassador is never recalled. But when five terrorists, who actually committed murder, were executed in Madrid, then the British ambassador *was* recalled and the din reverberated throughout the world. What a hurricane burst forth from the British Isles! You have to know how to protest, it has to be done with a great deal of anger, but only as long as it doesn't run counter to the spirit of the age and presents no danger to the authority of those protesting. If only you could make use of your British skepticism for a moment (it can't have deserted you entirely) and put yourselves in the position of the oppressed peoples of Eastern Europe—then you can view your unseemly behavior through our eyes! The Prime Minister of Spain was murdered and all cultured Europe was delighted. Some Spanish policemen, even some Spanish hairdressers, were murdered—and the countries of Europe went wild with joy, as if their own police were insured against the Terrorist International.

Not a single family driving to an airport can be sure that it won't be gunned down by some fighter for someone or other's freedom. No one can be sure that he'll get to the end of the street safe and sound. But terrorists can be sure: public opinion guarantees that *their* lives will be safe, that *their* cause will be given publicity, and that *they* will be held in decent confinement—that is, until other terrorists come and rescue them. A society for the protection of terrorists indeed! There *was* such a society in Russia before her collapse: we too have trodden this fatal path.

Meanwhile, the crevasse grows ever wider, spreads even farther across the globe, shifts into other continents. The most populous country in the world has plunged headlong into it. So have a dozen others. So, too, have numerous defenseless tribes—Kurds, Northern Abyssinians, Somalis, Angolans. And the British, with their great tradition of freedom, haven't the slightest anxiety over such petty matters. Even today you are lulled into thinking that these fine islands of yours will never be split in two by that crevasse, will never be blown sky-high. And yet the abyss is already there, beneath your very feet. Every year several more countries are seized and taken over as bridgeheads for the coming world war, and the whole world stands by and does nothing.

Even the oceans are being taken over, and need one tell you British what that means or what the seas will be used for? And what of Europe today? It is nothing more than a collection of cardboard stage sets, all bargaining with each other to see how little can be spent on defense in order to leave more for the comforts of life. The continent of Europe, with its centuries-long preparation for the task of leading mankind, has of its own accord abandoned its strength and its influence on world affairs—and not just its physical influence but its intellectual influence as well. Potentially important decisions, major movements, have now begun to mature beyond the frontiers of Europe. How strange it all is! Since when has mighty Europe needed outside help to defend herself? At one moment she had such a surfeit of strength that, while waging wars within her own boundaries and destroying herself, she was still able to seize colonies. A moment later, she suddenly found herself hopelessly weak without having lost a single major war.

However hidden it may be from human gaze, however unexpected for the practical mind, there is sometimes a direct link between the evil we cause to others and the evil which suddenly confronts us. Pragmatists may explain this link as a chain of natural cause and effect. But those who are more inclined to a religious view of life will immediately perceive a link between sin and punishment. It can be seen in the history of every country. Today's generation has had to pay for the shortcomings of their fathers and grandfathers, who blocked their ears to the lamentations of the world and closed their eyes to its miseries and disasters.

Your newspapers may be famous for their traditions, but they print a number of articles containing analyses and commentaries which are shamefully shallow and shortsighted. What *can* one say when your leading liberal paper compares the contemporary development of the Russian spiritual regeneration with pigs trying to fly? This is not just contempt for the spiritual potential of my people. It's broader than that. It's a kind of fastidious contempt for *any* kind of spiritual regeneration, for anything which does not stem directly from economics but which is based on moral criteria. What an inglorious end to four hundred years of materialism!

The decline of contemporary thought has been hastened by the misty phantom of socialism. Socialism has created the illusion of quenching people's thirst for justice: Socialism has lulled their conscience into thinking that the steamroller which is about to flatten them is a blessing in disguise, a salvation. And socialism, more than anything else, has caused public hypocrisy to thrive; it has enabled Europe to ignore the annihilation of 66 million people on its very borders.

There is not even a single precise definition of socialism that is generally recognized: all we have is a sort of hazy shimmering concept of something good, something noble, so that two socialists talking to each other about socialism might just as well be talking about completely different things. And, of course, any new-style African dictator can call himself a socialist without fear of contradiction.

But socialism defies logic. You see, it is an emotional impulse, a kind of worldly religion, and nobody has the slightest need to study or even to read the teachings of its early prophets. Their books are judged by hearsay; their conclusions are accepted ready-made. Socialism is defended with a passionate lack of reason; it is never analyzed; it's proof against all criticism. Socialism, especially Marxist socialism, uses the neat device of declaring all serious criticism "outside the framework of possible discussion"; and one is required to accept 95 percent of socialist doctrine as a "basis for discussion"—all that is left to argue about is the remaining 5 percent.

There is another myth here too, namely that socialism represents a sort of ultra-modern structure, an alternative to dying capitalism. And yet it existed ages and ages before any sort of capitalism.

My friend Academician Igor Shafarevich has shown in his extensive study of socialism that socialist *systems*, which are being used today to lure us to some halcyon future, made up the greatest portion of the previous history of mankind in the ancient East, in China, and were repeated later in the bloody experiments of the Reformation. As for socialist *doctrines,* he has shown that they emerged far later but have still been with us for over two thousand years; and that they originated not in an eruption of progressive thought as people think nowadays but as a reaction—Plato's reaction against Athenian democracy, the Gnostics' reaction against Christianity—against the dynamic world of individualism and as a return to the impersonal, stagnant system of antiquity. And if we follow the explosive sequence of socialist doctrines and socialist utopias preached in Europe—by Thomas More, Campanella, Winstanley, Morelli, Deschamps, Babeuf, Fourier, Marx, and dozens of others—we cannot help but shudder as they openly proclaim certain features of that terrible form of society. It is about time we called upon right-minded socialists calmly and without prejudice to read, say, a dozen of the major works of the major prophets of European socialism and to ask themselves: Is this *really* that social ideal for which they would be prepared to sacrifice the lives of countless others and even to sacrifice their own?

You imagine you see danger in other parts of the

globe and so you hurl the arrows from your depleted quiver there. But the greatest danger of all is that you have lost the will to defend yourselves.

Great Britain, the kernel of the Western world, has experienced this sapping of its strength and will to an even greater degree, perhaps, than any other country. For some twenty years Britain's voice has not been heard in our planet; its character has gone, its freshness has faded. And Britain's position in the world today is of less significance than that of Romania, or even . . . Uganda. British common sense—so lucid, so universally acknowledged—seems to have failed her now. Contemporary society in Britain is living on self-deception and illusions, both in the world of politics and in the world of ideas. People build rickety structures to convince themselves that there *is* no danger and that its irrevocable advance is nothing more than the establishment of a stable world.

We, the oppressed people of Russia, the oppressed people of Eastern Europe, watch with anguish the tragic enfeeblement of Europe. We offer you the experience of our suffering; we would like you to accept it without having to pay the monstrous price of death and slavery that we have paid. But your society refuses to heed our warning voices. I suppose we must admit, sad though it is, that experience cannot be transmitted: everyone must experience everything for himself.

Of course, it's not just a question of Britain; it's not just a question of the West—it concerns all of us, in the East as well as in the West. We are all, each in his own way, bound together by a common fate, by the same bands of iron. And all of us are standing on the brink of a great historical cataclysm, a flood that swallows up civilization and changes whole epochs. The present world situation is complicated still more by the fact that several hours have struck simultaneously on the clock of history. We all must face up to a crisis—not just a social crisis, not just a political crisis, not just a military crisis—face up to it, but also stand firm in this great upheaval, an upheaval similar to that which marked the transition from the Middle Ages to the Renaissance. Just as mankind once became aware of the intolerable and mistaken deviation of the late Middle Ages and recoiled in horror from it, so too must we take account of the disastrous deviation of the late Enlightenment. We have become hopelessly enmeshed in our slavish worship of all that is pleasant, all that is comfortable, all that is material—we worship things, we worship products.

Will we ever succeed in shaking off this burden, in giving free rein to the spirit that was breathed into us at birth, that spirit which distinguishes us from the animal world?